WAYNE SCHMIDT

FOREWORD BY JOHN MAXWELL

SOUL

MANAGEMENT

Maximizing Your Spiritual Assets in a Bottom-Line World

ZondervanPublishingHouse

Grand Rapids, Michigan

A Division of HarperCollins*Publishers*

Soul Management
Copyright © 1996 by Wayne Schmidt

Requests for information should be addressed to:

■ ZondervanPublishingHouse
Grand Rapids, Michigan 49530

Library of Congress Cataloging-in-Publication Data

Schmidt, Wayne, 1957–.
    Soul management: maximizing your spiritual assets in a bottom-line world /
Wayne Schmidt.
        p. cm.
    ISBN: 0-310-20102-0
    1. Bible. O.T. Ecclesiastes—Devotional use. 2. Spiritual life—Christianity. I.
Title.
BS1475.4.S35 1996
248.4-dc 20   95-40915
                                                                                        CIP

This edition printed on acid-free paper and meets the American National
Standards Institute Z39.48 standard.

Edited by Verlyn D. Verbrugge
Interior design by Sue Koppenol

Printed in the United States of America

96 97 98 99 00 01 02 03 /❖ DH/ 10 9 8 7 6 5 4 3 2 1

CONTENTS

Acknowledgments

In the process of writing I have appreciated anew the numerous individuals who by God's grace have influenced me toward the "bottom line" reflected in this book. I am blessed

- with a heritage of parents and grandparents who have hearts for God and for me
- with a marriage to Jan, whose patience and love prompted me to grow and change
- with three children–Chris, Jordan, and Elise–who deserve an earthly father who in some small way reflects their heavenly Father
- with a church family at Kentwood Community, led by a pastoral staff and lay leaders whose committed use of their spiritual gifts allows me to explore and utilize mine
- with an accountability partner, Paul Anthes, who for over a decade has been a true friend
- with mentors like Russ Mawby and Dick Wynn, models like John Maxwell, Bill Hardiman, and Jerry DeRuiter, and "marathoners" like Roland and Joyce Johnson, Bernice Hansen-Gilbert, and Delos Tanner

I have grown as a person in writing this book. Lyn Cryderman believed in me as began this opportunity. Verlyn Verbrugge sharpened my ideas, while a small group of men helped me to refine them in concept–Chuck Roost, Mike Perry, Bob Blanchard, Bill Genson, and Paul Anthes.

Most of all I wish to acknowledge Jesus Christ, without whom the "bottom line" of eternity is an impossibility.

Foreword

Every business person in America knows exactly what you mean when you talk about the bottom line: It's the final entry in the accounting ledger, the yardstick that measures profitability, the key indicator of a business's pending success or failure. The hopes and dreams of people live and die by the bottom line.

And if you ask a businessperson, he'll also tell you that the bottom line is a reflection of all the components that contribute to it. When those components are well managed, then the bottom line is good. When those components are weak or poorly managed, so is the bottom line. And when you want to improve the bottom line, you have to focus on the contributing factors, not on the bottom line itself. If you can manage small changes in those contributing areas and develop a series of minor successes throughout the ledger, it can create major success in the bottom line.

To many men in the working world, this is a simple truth they live with every day. But when those same men look outside of the business environment and begin searching for answers to some of life's deeper questions, especially questions pertaining to spiritual matters, they often lose touch with that truth. Or maybe they think it doesn't apply. But the reality is that bottom-line thinking can apply to every area of life, including a man's spiritual health and growth.

Wayne Schmidt understands bottom-line thinking, because he's a bottom-line person. In this book he touches on some of the toughest issues men face: money, priorities, decision making, relationships, commitment, balance, and death. And he looks at these issues with wisdom from one of the greatest bottom-line thinkers who ever lived– Solomon.

Solomon reached the pinnacle of success in every area of life. He ruled a nation ordained by God. He had wealth and power greater than any other man in the world of his time. He built cities. He was an accomplished artist who wrote music and poetry. He experienced everything that the world had to offer. He is said to have been the wisest man who ever lived. And when he wrote the book of Ecclesiastes, he measured the value of his life and its works. Now that's bottom-line thinking!

Join with Wayne as he shares insights on what it means to be a bottom-line man in your spiritual life. The journey is worth taking, because the real bottom line is that when you order your life according to God's accounting system, it leads to true top of the line living.

John Maxwell
INJOY
San Diego, CA

1

Life: Treadmill or Pathway?

SCRIPTURE: ECCLESIASTES 1:1–11

I am a bottom-line person. By nature I am focused, intense, and task-oriented. I am most comfortable when I am accomplishing something that yields tangible results. As a young man I dreamed of being a real estate developer. I was attracted to the idea of creating something that would benefit others – and myself. I was enamored with the potential risks and rewards.

God had something else in mind. I had my plans, but he had his. We entered into a battle of wills. After months of misery, God won and I lost. But like so many other men, I discovered "losing out" to God's will is the ultimate form of victory. He really does know what is best.

I envisioned developing property; God envisioned my developing people. I anticipated an earthly payoff; God provided a spiritual harvest. So in the mid 1970s, I submitted to his desire that I enter pastoral ministry.

I am a pastor, but I am still a bottom-line person. While God changed the focus of my efforts, I did not change my approach to life. I thought he valued me because of what I could do for him. I worked harder and longer, attempting to prove my worth by my performance. The church I have been involved with since its beginning grew dramatically. Church growth awards filled the wall of our boardroom. The congregation increased to over one thousand before I was thirty. But the alarms inside me began to sound. More and more was happening around me, but less and less was happening within me. There was an emptiness inside that few who knew me professionally would have ever expected.

I was a classic man of the 90s. My "cool and calm" exterior masked an increasingly chaotic interior. I was a workaholic, and each day I was becoming more of a human doing and less of a human being.

Gradually I awakened to my condition. There was the love of my wife creating a hunger in me for a more intimate relationship with her. There were the needs of my children, at risk of growing up with an emotionally, if not physically, absent father. There was the prodding of my accountability partner, reinforcing my as yet unfulfilled desire for some balance in life. There was the death of my father, causing me to reflect on what life is really all about.

Has my external life changed dramatically? Not in the eyes of people who know me casually. I still lead that same dynamic church that is reaching the community and now literally around the world. I am still a bottom-line person, as God created me to be. I grew up in a church tradition that seemed to identify spirituality with a certain kind of personality—one I didn't have! I have since discovered that my intensity was God's idea. His will is not for me to cease being a "bottom-line" person, but rather to choose the bottom line of life carefully and define it clearly.

The difference is my inner world has come alive! My view of my quiet times has changed from being a performance review ("How am I doing, God?") to sharing life with my Creator ("I want to know you, God"). My commitments to date my wife and spend time with my kids have created a deep longing for more of a relationship shaped by eternal perspectives. These and other changes create a bottom line that fills the soul.

One of the great advantages of being a pastor is the privilege of going behind the scenes in the lives of so many men. They talk to me about subjects that are off-limits in so many "guy conversations." They reveal their spiritual doubts, their family concerns, their struggles with life's meaning. I get to share vicariously in their successes. I witness the consequences of their choices. I see the common mistakes, watch them fall, and then watch them grow.

I see a trend in those behind-the-scenes interactions with men. They don't want to miss out on the best in life by spending time on things of lesser value. Many feel they have been living on autopilot or cruise control. They want to raise the standard of their personal and spiritual lives, but fear that taking it up a notch will only mean a longer to-do list. They are often too tired to work harder. Instead, they want to access greater resources. They want the next years of their lives to be the best years. I identify with their life stories because they resonate with my life story. Maybe you know those feelings too.

There's a book in the Bible that gives us a behind-the-scenes glimpse into the life of a bottom-line man. Called Ecclesiastes, it reads like a journal. You may struggle to grasp some of his illustrations, but his message is loud and clear. Listen to his opening words:

"Meaningless! Meaningless!"
  says the Teacher.
"Utterly meaningless!
  Everything is meaningless."

What does man gain from all his labor
  at which he toils under the sun?
Generations come and generations go,
  but the earth remains forever.
The sun rises and the sun sets,
  and hurries back to where it rises.
The wind blows to the south
  and turns to the north;
round and round it goes,
  ever returning on its course.
All streams flow into the sea,
  yet the sea is never full.
To the place the streams come from,
  there they return again.
All things are wearisome,
  more than one can say.
The eye never has enough of seeing,
  nor the ear its fill of hearing.
What has been will be again,
  what has been done will be done again;
  there is nothing new under the sun.
Is there anything of which one can say,
  "Look! This is something new!"
It was here already, long ago;
  it was here before our time.
There is no remembrance of men of old,
  and even those who are yet to come
will be not be remembered
  by those who follow.

The author is asking the tough questions:

Verse 3: *"What does man gain from all his labor?"*
He's wondering what the payoff is for all of his hard work.
Verse 10: *"Is there anything of which one can say, 'Look! This is something new?'"*
If his first question centers around his efforts, this one centers around his experiences: What's new to say, to see, to hear?

I've heard these questions again and again from men in different life situations. I also hear similar conclusions:

Verse 2: *"Everything is meaningless."* (I'm empty.)
Verse 8: *"All things are wearisome."* (I'm tired.)
Verse 8: *"Never . . . enough."* (I'm restless.)
Verse 11: *"There is no remembrance."* (I'm expendable.)

The author concludes that life is a treadmill. Even the breaks – the vacations, toys, sex, travel – do not bring lasting satisfaction.

Don't miss the one little phrase that reveals his paradigm: "under the sun." "What does a man gain from all his labor . . . *under the sun?*" "There is nothing new *under the sun.*" That's the author's way of saying God is not yet in the picture. He has not yet integrated his relationship with God into the experiences of life. His dissatisfaction launches him on a search to discover how God's will intersects with his world. He is seeking the little steps that lead to an "above-the-sun," top of the line approach to life.

I invite you to join me on a journey through his journal. Take an honest look at where you have been, where you are, and where you are going. Listen to the Teacher's words with both your mind and your heart. Learn from his experiences in order to prepare yourself for this life and beyond. You will discover the difference between those men whose efforts and experiences leave them empty and those who discover they are on the pathway to meaning.

There is a formula that serves as a map for our journey with him. It is a formula uncovered by management gurus decades ago that outlines the process of change.

$$D \times V \times F > R$$
Dissatisfaction x Vision x First Steps > Resistance

This model contends that if lasting, meaningful change is to occur, Dissatisfaction (D) with the way things are now, a Vision (V) of how we would like them to be, and commitment to some realistic First Steps (F) must be greater than Resistance (R) to change. If any variable on the left side of the equation (D, V, or F) is zero (that is, there is no dissatisfaction with the present, no vision for the future, or no first steps in an action plan), then all three equal zero. It is then impossible to change, because there is always resistance to do so.

Let's take a closer look at the variables.

DISSATISFACTION

An acquaintance of mine had a dream job. He traveled by corporate jet to some of the most glamorous locations around the world. Limousines awaited his arrival, transporting him to suites in some of the finest hotels. There he enjoyed sumptuous meals with some of the most beautiful, positive people in the world. One day he said to me, "Wayne, I'm in a dream world of success and prosperity; I'm surrounded by stimulating people in a first-class environment. Yet my mind is elsewhere. I'm smiling on the outside, but inside I just want to be home with my family."

What's wrong with that picture? Nothing, until you look behind the scenes and see the dissatisfaction. Mick Jagger sings, "I Can't Get No Satisfaction," and Jackson Browne, "Running on Empty." Pat Williams, General Manager of the Orlando Magic, calls it the "emptiness after initial exertion," where men in the high-powered world of sports find that fortune, fame, and power are not enough. Bob Buford labels it as "questioning and self-doubt." These people are all putting a finger on that sense of quiet desperation in the hearts of men.

In a society that has attained so much and where so many experiences are available, are men happier? Is there more peace of mind, more meaning in life? Some argue there is more dissatisfaction than ever! They feel a nagging sense that their lives are mediocre, that they are stuck in the status quo. For some men it's a dissonance in their hearts as they experience the incredible pain of life (relationships, careers, etc.) not turning out as they had pictured. And this is not just a midlife issue, for every year it seems to be hitting men at younger ages.

How do men respond to these signals that something is missing? Some deny it, suppressing the feelings until they can endure them no longer. Others marinate in it, paralyzed by a sense of hopelessness that things can never be different. Still others reorder their external world, as if a new job (or wife or geographical location or . . .) will address the emptiness they feel inside.

I am learning to value it, and I would encourage you to do the same. As we acknowledge our sense of meaninglessness, we are motivated to search for more. We must learn to value emptiness for its positive potential. As an empty cup invites water or a vacant room invites entrance, so an empty heart can lead us to search for God-given ways to fill it.

Dissatisfaction is the diagnosis phase that impels us to ask, "What's wrong here?" In organizational development there is a truism that "prescription without diagnosis is malpractice, whether it be in medicine or in management." I would add, "whether it be in medicine or in discovering meaning in life."

> Emptiness is at the center of our humanness. To flee it is to miss the creative openness toward creation and the Creator. To stuff it full of things is to block our ability to receive others in listening love. To anesthetize it with addictive experiences is to deaden the creative springs of the true self. Emptiness is to be embraced as a gift.[1]

Dissatisfaction is not the finish line, it is the starting block. It is where the writer of Ecclesiastes launches his search.

VISION

The quest for meaning is inspired by the need to connect life to something larger. For most of human history, no one had to search for God or the sacred, for it was assumed to be the real world. That is no longer true. Now the "under the sun" secular world is scientifically validated as real. Yet people are seeking something transcendent as never before. Ray Lanson identifies it as the "astrodome effect":

> Living in a secular world is like living in an astrodome with a roof over the top. The temperature is always 70 and the grass is always green. Even in a place that holds 70,000 people, you feel claustrophobic. You need to breathe some fresh air.[2]

Vision is the fresh air of meaning. Ecclesiastes gives us just glimpses along the way, and that is realistic. In this life we never get the whole picture but learn to live by faith and trust.

The author assumes the identity of a secularist, which is the beginning point for so many men. He first exhausts all this life has to offer "under the sun" before looking up. God initially seems distant to him, unreal and disconnected from everyday life. He focuses on what he can create rather than on acknowledging the Creator. He eventually perceives that everything is meaningless if God is not in the picture and that we must link the activity of this life to the eternal purposes of God.

In the end, the author will urge us to "remember your Creator in the days of your youth" (12:1). This is his way of saying, "Don't make God the last thing you reach for. Don't start by thinking how you are going to solve it, which self-help book you need, or which consultant you should seek. Don't go to God as a last resort, leaving him the leftovers so that his work in your life can be nothing more than a rescue mission. Seek God ASAP; you'll never be younger than you are today."

"Do-it-yourself" will never get it done. You need a vertical vision that ultimately connects all you are and all you do with the person of Jesus Christ. Without his strength and guidance, your efforts to change are just another burden, something else you feel you are not doing right. You will then feel more guilt rather than experience his life-transforming grace.

Vision will always be a work in progress. In the words of one man recovering from alcoholism: "Is just 'not taking a drink' a high enough purpose in living? What do you want out of your sobriety?" To paraphrase the question: "Is contentment enough? What do you want to accomplish for your own well-being, the good of others, and the glory of

God?" That is vertical vision, and you will get glimpses of it throughout your life journey.

FIRST STEPS

A vision without realistic first steps is a daydream, nothing more than a good idea for a vague "someday." First steps form the action plan, the bite-size pieces of vision that we can swallow. Like the first steps of a baby, they may falter. We feel vulnerable and will probably sit down hard on more than one occasion. The journal of Ecclesiastes exposes the areas we struggle with—continual learning, time management, relationships, and making and keeping our commitments. The chapters of this book target those areas as well and include ways in which we can integrate our vertical vision with everyday life.

For instance, take the desire for a meaningful marriage relationship. Most men now come from homes broken by divorce or where their parents simply negotiated a truce rather than created a relationship. They know what they don't want their marriages to be like (dissatisfaction). If they have studied what the Bible says, they know what their marriages should ideally be like (vision), such as a man loving his wife as Christ loved the church (Ephesians 5:25). But building a marriage requires more than lofty aspirations. It requires daily actions. It means being sure you date your wife, listen to her, pray with her, and surprise her with simple expressions of thoughtfulness. The cumulative effect of these little endeavors sets the tone of your marriage.

So it is with every area of life. First steps, one after another, shape the course of your life.

RESISTANCE

Personal growth should come easily and naturally, but it doesn't. Why not? Because any attempt to alter the status quo will meet with resistance. If there is no resistance, there has been no change. And even if the change is right, expect resistance.

At times that resistance comes from within you. I experienced that as I attempted to overcome my workaholism. I had always measured my value by what I did. I resisted a new standard of measurement, namely, what God was doing in me. Was I dissatisfied with the impact of workaholism on my life? Yes. Did I have a vision for something more? Just glimpses at the beginning. Did I know what some of the first steps were? I was becoming aware of them. But I am moving beyond my cautiously controlled comfort zone into a way of life I know little about. I will have to live with some ambiguity and uncertainty as a result of my personal paradigm shift. I can relate to the observation of an acquaintance who told me, "You can tell the area where change is being made because of the claw marks all over everything!"

Other times resistance comes from around you. People may have a vested interest in your staying the way you are. I have sat with a family during an "intervention," a session in which their husband and father was confronted with the impact of his alcoholism—and I later witnessed their subtle sabotage of his attempts to change. Even though the old patterns were painful, they were at least familiar. I have listened to a wife bemoan her husband's travel schedule but resist any attempt at change that might limit his career. Her identity rested in her position as "the wife of a successful executive." Advertisers are constantly seeking to convince you that their product will provide meaning "under the sun." Cultural distortions of truth paint commitment as restrictive and spiritual life as acceptable only if it makes little difference in what you say or do.

Our journey through Ecclesiastes may prompt some personal paradigm shifts for you. Some areas of your life may require nothing more than a minor tune-up, so there will be little resistance. Other areas may need a major overhaul. Most men I know don't address these areas until there is a crisis, or perhaps a series of crises. They may be discontented with how things are, but lots of people are discontent and yet not ready to take the risk of doing something about it. I have heard it takes 42 to 45 commercials to get a person to be open to a new product. I invite you to be open to the Teacher in Ecclesiastes, even if it requires 42 to 45 glimpses of a vision for how your life can be more meaningful.

THE BOTTOM LINE

What is a bottom line?

- It's a way of measuring success and effectiveness. In a business setting it is identifying the right focus (sales quotas, balance sheet, etc.) and the right time frames (monthly, quarterly, annually, etc.).
- It's a way of describing a person who is focused and intense. Their measurements of success tend to be more tangible than relational.
- It's a statement of truth, a core value, a foundational and nonnegotiable belief.
- It's the final offer after a person has cut through the fluff and identified the best he will do.
- It's a way of summing it all up, of giving the conclusion of the matter.

If you are a bottom-line man, you need to know that Ecclesiastes will not say, "Stop being bottom line." It will challenge you to choose your bottom line carefully and define it clearly. It will deal with life's toughest issues. It is not a candy-coated approach to human existence, attempting to mask the darker characteristics of manhood like selfishness, hypocrisy, oppression, untimely death, or injustice. It will tell it like it is.

If we are on a journey, we have a destination. Many Americans are spiritual tourists, so in love with the search that they have lost a sense of destination. Unless you are sightseeing, the purpose of every journey is to arrive where you want to be, where God wants you to be.

The author of Ecclesiastes has something to say to all of us. Maybe you are initially seeking a relationship with God. Perhaps you are dutifully religious. Or you have walked with God for years and desire to keep integrating your relationship with God into every dimension of your life. No matter where your search begins, he will offer something worth finding.

There is a danger for any business that tracks the wrong bottom line or fails to prioritize in areas where various bottom lines compete. Taking the wrong measurements can jeopardize that business's future well-being. This is true in personal life as well. What is the real bottom line in a world that promises more and more, yet delivers less and less? God's guidelines will yield lasting results.

NOTES

1. David Augsburger, *When Enough Is Enough* (Ventura, Calif.: Regal Books, 1984), p. 52.

2. "In Search of the Sacred,"*Newsweek* (November 28, 1994), p. 53.

2

Ignorance Is Bliss?

SCRIPTURE: ECCLESIASTES 1:12–18

- Everyone is talking about it, and daily news stories highlight its development.
- It can take us anywhere in the world we want to go.
- We all will travel it, though we are not sure where it will lead us.
- No two people navigate it at the same speed.
- It costs billions of dollars, with companies and governments staking their whole futures on it.
- It will never be completed, and parts of it are becoming outdated as it is being constructed.

It is known as "The Superhighway," and it is changing our lives. It takes shape as the computer "lane" increasingly parallels the communication "lane," and we are learning how to "change lanes." This interactive technology is leading us into a new frontier, envisioned to bring its developers greater fortunes than those that accompanied the building of railroads, mining of gold, or drilling for oil.

How is this information explosion transforming your life? A computer may not be a necessary tool of your trade, indispensable to your job performance. On the other hand, technology may have allowed your company to downsize, changing or eliminating your job. One thing is certain: More knowledge is available than ever before:

> Fifty percent of all the scientists who ever lived are alive today.
> Fifty percent of all the discoveries in natural science have been made in this century.
> Fifty percent of all the books ever written were written in the last 50 years.
> Fifty percent of the knowledge known by medical doctors was unknown just 20 years ago; Ninety percent of all that is known by medical doctors was unknown 70 years ago.
> All of us have access to 100 times as much music as anyone had before Thomas Edison invented the phonograph.
> We travel 100 times as much per year as our ancestors did a century ago.[1]

The prophets of this information age contend it has only just begun. Some estimate we now have available to us less than 20 percent of what will be available by 2010.

I don't often ponder the enormity of these changes, but I see them all around me. My car's manufacturer has spent more money on its electronics than its steel. I leave messages on someone's voice mail every day. I needed a training session just to use the phone on my desk. My wife works out of our home, thanks to desktop publishing. And it has only just begun!

We need to update our hardware and get the latest version of software. But we need also to use our "wetware."

Wetware? That's the label given by some "techno-weenies" to the gray matter between our ears—our brains!

To thrive in today's society you must become a lifelong learner. As adults we learn on a need-to-know basis, and every day there are more facts and skills that we must know. Colleges and universities are targeting "intermittent learners"—adults who reenter the learning environment at various stages of their careers in order to gain a new skill or obtain a newly necessary degree.

Technology has also become part of our "search for the sacred." New York's Cardinal John O'Connor fields questions from the public via computer. The online service CompuServe has offered a religious forum since the late 1980s. On the Internet you can locate Bible study groups, advice on meditation, or exploration in New Age philosophy.

I think the author of Ecclesiastes would have been frustrated with the Information Age. On the one hand he prided himself on knowledge (1:16) and was a devoted student with broad interests (1:12). On the other hand, however, he recognized that the quest for knowledge can be as empty as chasing the wind. The relentless pursuit of data can be numbing, leaving one oblivious to the true meaning of life. How does a person benefit from the pro-liferation of information, yet live life deeply and fully? I suggest three things.

1. *Value intuition.* Do not allow your quest for data to thwart the development of good instincts: the "knowing in your heart" what might be best. In equipping couples for marriage or teams of people to work together, I often use the Personal Dynamics Profile (PDP). It measures certain personality traits, but also indicates whether a person tends to rely on facts or trust feelings when making decisions. That is not always easy to detect, since some make decisions

intuitively and then line up the supporting data so as to appear "factual."

The PDP indicates that the one method of decision making is not necessarily better than the other. You can make a dumb decision after gathering reams of data. Yet proper research can keep you from a decision with negative implications for yourself and others. And sometimes the best decisions are made by ignoring the information collected and going on intuition.

Wisdom is found in developing an appreciation for both. I know a successful businessman who is as factual as they come. As often happens in marriage, opposites attract, and his spouse relies on intuition. As they have grown together, he has learned to trust her feelings and will not make a final decision in his business unless she "senses" it is right. He does not require her to articulate the factual foundation for her conclusions, though he does encourage her to explore the sources of her feelings. When his facts are in line with her feelings, together they make the wise choices that have allowed them to prosper.

Do not allow society to condition you to be factual to the detriment of a healthy sense of intuition. A good "gut check" can increase the possibility of a wise decision.

2. *Give your mind a break.* Does your mind get the necessary downtime? Your pursuit of information and the ready availability of communication may keep your "wetware" from ever resting.

To its credit, the *Wall Street Journal* regularly carries articles attempting to assess the impact of the workplace on personal and family development. In a recent interview, Karen Walker, Compaq's vice-president of operating services, expressed alarm when faxes from her staff began arriving in the middle of the night. "People are now thinking and working on the job twelve to eighteen hours a day," she says, adding that she limits her own hours to try to provide an example. When she travels and finds an employee voice mail on the phone in her hotel room at 11 P.M., she explains, "I send them an e-mail that says, 'Shouldn't you be doing something else at this hour?'" She has asked two employees in the last three months to cut their hours. "Your mind," she told them, "has to have some down time."[2]

Deeper levels of thinking are incompatible with a racing, tired mind. Have values like a good night's sleep become undesirable (or even guilt-producing) in a productivity-driven world? Don't allow the motion of life to deprive you of the meaning of life.

3. *Know what you need to know.* There is no doubt that we know more, or at least have the capability of knowing more today. Peter Drucker, America's preeminent management writer, has looked intensively at the link between business productivity and infoliteracy. He challenges CEOs to learn to take "information responsibility" by asking questions such as, "What information do I need to do my job? When do I need it? From whom do I need it? What information do I owe to others?" In other words, it is not knowing more but knowing what is necessary that makes the difference.

Compared to your counterpart from even one generation ago, you know much more. Riding the information highway is indispensable to career success. But do you know what you need to so that you can relate effectively to your wife, your children, and your God? Are you happier, more at peace, and more contented than your father? This is where hardware and software encounter their limits. This is where your God-given "wetware" enables you to do your best thinking.

REFLECTION

It is obvious from Ecclesiastes that other kinds of "knowing" unfold the deeper meaning of life. The pursuit of information is necessary, but not all-sufficient. Notice these entries in the Teacher's journal:

I thought to myself. (1:16)
I thought in my heart. (2:15)
I said in my heart. (2:15)

The words "I" and "my" are prominent. He is looking within, consulting with himself. There is no evidence that he talked to himself, yet that is a conversation we need to have! His head is in dialogue with his heart.

The most critical knowledge for your career in the new economy may turn out to be self-knowledge.

> The key to success, perhaps even to survival, in the new world is, pardon the already too familiar expression, lifelong learning. For managers and executives, the most painful learning–like knowing thyself–may prove the most valuable.[5]

The bombardment of external information can prevent you from taking a good long look inside. It can be a lot more comfortable to stare into a computer screen than into a mirror.

A friend of mine is a residential builder and developer. He acquires property he believes has the potential for development–providing attractive home sites without incurring prohibitive costs. He often secures the property with an option while he investigates its value.

Part of his investigation involves soil borings. He must test for contaminants since properties that appear to be ideal may be worthless as a result of the liability of environmental pollution. Soil borings also reveal the depth of the water table and the type of soil, both of which impact the ease and cost of development. In discussing this process with me, he said something I will never forget: "The potential for development has everything to do with what lies beneath the surface." And so it is with us. What lies beneath the surface of your life? Who are you? Why has God permitted certain experiences to enter your life?

My understanding of my purpose in life has grown through reflection. I "think to myself" about how people and experiences I have encountered may serve to prepare me for my future. In some areas I am fairly certain why things have happened; in others I am still searching.

As a child, I took piano lessons for seven long years (they must have seemed even longer to my mother!). In spite of the combined efforts of my piano teacher and mother, I never caught on. Even though I did not understand the music, I still had to perform the piece (for a very limited audience, for obvious reasons). I got by through memorization. My memory developed, my musical ability did not. Today I cannot play a note. The question I have since asked: Why seven years of lessons? Is there nothing to show for it?

Many newcomers visit our church each week. One of their first impressions is the quality and variety of our music program. Another is that I do not use a pulpit or notes, speaking only from memory. Where did a vision for a ministry that places a high priority on music develop? Where did I develop that memory? Is there any connection with seven long years on a piano bench? Reflection helps you link past experiences with the formation of your life's purpose.

Reflection also enables you to break the cycle of dysfunctional behavior. Let's face it, none of us is 100 percent "functional." We all have qualities we would rather not pass on to our children. How you treat your children may well be related to how your father treated you and his father treated him. The blessings you derive from that generational cycle should be received with thanksgiving. Behaviors that are harmful need not be repeated. You are not simply a creature of habit. Through personal reflection or the skills of a counselor who helps you to reflect, you can choose to chart a different course. Often "unlearning" is as important as learning. Be a lifelong "unlearner" as well as lifelong learner.

Reflection presses meaning into life. Here are a few guidelines:

1. *Beware of distortion.* Have you ever been in a house of mirrors? Some make you look fat, some skinny. Some add inches to your height, others take it away. Because you have previously looked in regular mirrors, you recognize the distortion in your reflection. The reflection fundamental to self-knowledge can also be distorted, though it is not always recognized.

An anorexic girl looks in the mirror and thinks that she is fat as she starves herself to death. An alcoholic, bouncing between self-pride when drinking and self-loathing when sober, finds it nearly impossible to "know himself." Scripture makes it abundantly clear that the heart is capable of deceit. Reflection is the starting line, not the finish line, of self-knowledge. In the words of Winston Churchill during World War II, "The great thing is to get the true picture, whatever it is."[4]

2. *Reflection involves both your head and your heart.* That is, reflection means both thinking and feeling. Most men have been conditioned to emphasize the head and de-emphasize the heart. Ask not only, "What do I think of that experience?" but, "How does it make me feel?"

3. *Don't lock in prematurely on your conclusions.* Knowing yourself is a moving target! It is dangerous to put people in a box; it is equally dangerous to put yourself in a box.

4. *Be alert to teachable moments.* Bob Buford, in his book *Half Time*, identifies midlife as a great time for reflection. If you are not there yet, don't wait! If you feel you are past it, don't think you have missed your opportunity. There are many moments in life that can teach you something important about yourself.

- Right after a big achievement
- During a relaxed vacation
- Following a major disappointment
- Through reading a good book or listening to a tape
- Experiencing another culture
- Having a conversation or confrontation

As soon as possible, build time for reflection into your life.

5. *Add to your individual reflection regular interaction with others.* My accountability partner and I meet every two weeks. In addition to monitoring each other's goals, we discuss what is going on in our "private world." I share what I am learning about myself, and he does the same. A trusted friend who knows you well is a valuable resource in refining your perspectives.

6. *The best reflection is done in prayer.* During my quiet times, I regularly repeat the desire that Jesus, teaching his followers to pray, encouraged them to say to God, "Your kingdom come. *Your will be done. . . .*" I personalize that desire with the following statements:

- *Your will be done* in me physically—how am I caring for my body?
- *Your will be done* in me mentally—how am I developing my mind?

- *Your will be done* in me emotionally–am I angry? agitated? at peace?
- *Your will be done* in me relationally–am I building friendships? loving others?
- *Your will be done* in my relationship with my wife–is there anything I need to make right? Have I been investing time and energy in her?
- *Your will be done* in my relationship with my children–how is my communication with them?
- *Your will be done* in me spiritually–how is God at work in me?

This practice alerts me to the consequences of my choices.

Reflection is an indispensable ingredient in a meaningful life, though too much can do more harm than good. The introspection that helps us look beneath the surface must be coupled with a spirit of exploration that takes us beyond our comfort zones.

EXPLORATION

The writer of Ecclesiastes describes another dimension of life's learning curve: "I devoted myself to study and to *explore* by wisdom all that is done under heaven" (1:13). An explorer is someone who is interested in territory beyond the familiar, beyond where he has been before, beyond what he has already experienced.

Peter Drucker compares the need of an effective company for information to the wings of an airplane. One wing is called "inside information," the other "outside information."[5] In the same way, an effective person needs both inside information (coming from reflection) and outside information (coming from exploration) in order to "soar" to the highest possible levels of personal development. Knowing what you do not know can be even more important than knowing what you know; it motivates you to explore.

The operative word with exploration is willingness— to move beyond familiar territory and to face what you do not know. You need a willingness to ask for help. As men, admitting we are lost and asking for directions do not come easily or naturally. Driving is one example. When we encounter unfamiliar territory and someone suggests that we are lost, we do not stop and ask for directions; we just increase the speed. The only outcome is going the wrong way faster!

Our willingness to learn from others increases when we are "under pressure." At the Center for Creative Leadership in Greensboro, North Carolina, David Noer observes: "Adults don't learn unless they need to, *but under some pressure*—like the chance of getting a promotion or of keeping one's job—they can learn or be taught how to."[6]

"But under some pressure." I have seen that pressure build in various places:

- A marriage that has rolled along for years but suddenly is not going so well; the pressure created either drives a couple apart or motivates them to learn new communication skills
- A dad whose kids are growing from childhood to adolescence and seem to be growing away from him; he either watches the distance increase or learns to build bridges
- A man who can no longer control his anger, which alternately seethes and explodes; he sees his relationships wither or seeks counsel to disarm this volatile force.

I am puzzled by something. It seems that men are quicker to respond to workplace "pressure" than to relationship "pressure." Many men who are proactive in resolving career-based challenges are hopelessly passive at home. Though eager students with high energy to make a difference in their companies, they leave their learning and leadership capacities at the office. Are we better students of our business plans than our spouses? Do we know our management team better than our children? Don't let pressure build to the explosion point before focusing your attention. That may be too late.

Here are some trail markers for moving beyond yourself and familiar territory:

1. *Seek input from others.* Personal growth is accelerated by enlisting the perspectives of others. Some companies facilitate this process by conducting 360-degree evaluations. A person is evaluated by his supervisor—that has been done for years. But he is also evaluated by his fellow team members, his peers. An additional evaluation is given by the people who report to him. Such evaluations may include both professional performance and personal habits. Now that's exploring with the help of others! Conduct your own 360-degree evaluation—and be sure to include your wife and your children!

2. *Look for both strengths and weaknesses.* In the process of exploration you may be pleasantly surprised with the discovery of some strengths you have overlooked. You may be faced with some weaknesses that must be addressed. That may be unsettling, throwing you off balance. A bit of disequilibrium can open the door for needed change.

3. *Ask God for needed insight.* I am impressed with the search for knowledge that we have seen in this journal called Ecclesiastes. But it has all been done with one great limitation: "I devoted myself to study and explore by wisdom

all that is done *under heaven*" (1:13). "I have seen all the things that are done *under the sun*"(1:14).

The Teacher's search failed to include in any meaningful way the "wisdom that comes from above," the eternal perspective that only God can reveal. He deliberately excluded God, except to complain about the "heavy burden God has laid on men" (1:13). Is your prayer time a visit to the complaint department or to the information center? Sensitivity to God's Spirit helps you transcend the limits of self-knowledge.

The searcher concludes: "For with much wisdom comes much sorrow; the more knowledge, the more grief" (1:18). This sounds remarkably similar to aphorisms such as: "What you don't know can't hurt you"; or "Ignorance is bliss"; or "It's better to plead ignorance." He does admit to some advantages of knowledge: "The wise man has eyes in his head while the fool walks in darkness"; but even then he observes: "The same fate overtakes them both" (2:14). Apart from an "above the sun" perspective that includes God and eternity, there is little lasting value found in lifelong learning.

We resist the Teacher's pessimism, and yet we must take a good long look at the impact of knowing more. We must face the reality that all the information we have has not basically changed us:

- We spend millions on AIDS awareness, yet people who "know better" regularly engage in promiscuous sex.
- We have more consultants and experts in business than ever before, yet bankruptcies continually occur.
- We have learned about fat grams and exercise plans, yet bulges around the middle remain.

- Books on parenting and marriage appear regularly, yet families seem to struggle as never before.
- With all our knowledge, is there less violence? more hope? more peace and contentment?

We need more than information. *We need transformation.* The bottom line is this: "You must continually learn what you truly need to know, recognizing that learning has not taken place until your living has changed." And the highest level of learning has not taken place until your heart is changed, and then your behavior will be changed.

Life's most important learning curve relates to the "wisdom from above." We need men who know not only themselves, their spouses, their children, but their God and his wisdom and purposes for life. We need men with *pure* hearts, *peaceable* relationships, *gentle* demeanors, and *reasonable* minds. We need the wisdom that transforms our minds (Romans 12:2) and lifts our eyes "above the sun."

NOTES

1. Observations by Sir John Templeton, *Templeton Newsletter*, 1989.

2. *Wall Street Journal* (August 17, 1994).

3. Quote from Walter Kiechel III, *Fortune Magazine* (April 4, 1994), p. 70.

4. *Leadership Journal* (Winter 1995).

5. Peter Drucker, "Infoliteracy," *Forbes ASAP* (August 29, 1994), p. 108.

6. *Fortune* (April 4, 1994).

3

What's Your Pleasure?

An intriguing opportunity I have as a pastor is getting "behind the scenes" in a variety of men's lives. Beyond the surface symptoms of problems or the external perks of success, I converse with them about core issues, such as motivations—the bottom line of why they do what they do and choose what they choose.

A frequent response to the question "Why?" is the answer, "I just want to be happy." I hear it as people enter marriages. I hear it as people exit marriages. It is the reason given for changing jobs, or changing churches, or changing spouses.

There is no doubt that we are a pleasure-seeking society. Many people devote greater effort to planning leisure activities than to producing on the job. Entertainment is big business. Whether it is a million dollars spent to build the stage and props for a Rolling Stones concert or a million dollars spent to purchase an advertisement during the Super Bowl, the entertainment industry is the place to invest in order to capture America's attention. No wonder sports is an eleven billion dollar pastime, and it is merely one approach to quench our thirst for pleasure.

I often encounter a puzzling paradox, however. As men, we long to be happy, and we are capable of being selfish to satisfy that longing. I find myself agreeing with observations like, "Adults are babies with big bodies." In our weaker moments, we assume that others exist simply to meet our needs and relieve our discomfort.

But here is the head-scratcher: Many pleasure-seekers turn into pleasure-saboteurs just as happiness is within their grasp. As one businessman shared with me, "I seem to play the devil's advocate with happiness. Whenever my business reaches or exceeds its goals, I convince myself that it's never enough. When a dating relationship begins to go well, I whisper to myself that it won't last. Every time I build a foundation for happiness, I undermine it."

The author of Ecclesiastes was enamored with pleasure, recording these words in his journal one day: "I thought in my heart, 'Come now, I will test you with pleasure to find out what is good'" (2:1). He is going to test the relationship between seeking pleasure and discovering meaning in life.

ATTITUDE CHECK

The Teacher's pleasure test begins with well-managed curiosity. He is going to try some things and see if any satisfaction results from these experiences. He claims he will not get carried away, for wisdom will be his guiding light.

We are created with a natural sense of curiosity, the evidence of which is seen early in life. Babies are always searching for something to put into their mouths. The parental warning "Don't touch" makes a child want it even more! Children for decades have loved the stories of "Curious George," the monkey whose mischievous spirit of adventure lands him in all sorts of predicaments. We may be neither a monkey nor a George, but we are curious.

Teens display that innate sense of curiosity as well. It motivates them to experiment with alcohol, to engage in sexual activity, to risk taking a drug, or to go a hundred miles an hour in an automobile. Just being curious!

As adults we may be more sophisticated in disguising our curiosity, but we do not outgrow it. A healthy sense of curiosity keeps us growing and changing. Uncontrolled curiosity, on the other hand, can lead to choices that bear devastating consequences.

As the author of Ecclesiastes seeks for pleasure, his attitude begins subtly to change:

Well-Managed ⟶ Curiosity	Self-Indulgent Sensuality
I thought in my heart, "Come now, I will test you with pleasure to find out what is good." (2:1)	I denied myself nothing my eyes desired; I refused my heart no pleasure. (2:10)

Somewhere on his journey, as pleasurable experiments and experiences begin to accumulate, an "I deserve" mentality emerges. "I deserve any pleasure I want and shouldn't deny myself anything. I should follow my heart, not refuse its desires" (cf. 2:10).

It all starts innocently enough. You conclude, "I deserve a vacation," or "I deserve to knock off from work early today." Advertising is more than willing to encourage an entitlement mentality: "You deserve a break today" (from cooking and that low fat diet!). You deserve to be seen driving in a car like this, or taking a vacation like that. And maybe we do.

But this attitude, left unchecked, presents problems. One potential side effect is tension in a marriage. Imagine you are working hard. As the afternoon wears on, you envision getting home and easing back in your recliner. You see yourself with your nose in the newspaper, while delicious aromas emanate from the kitchen as your wife prepares your favorite meal. She, on the other hand, has also worked hard all day. She would like to see you fix the dinner (or take her out to eat). Your "I deserve" collides with her "I deserve." The tension escalates because an "I deserve" mentality causes a person to focus in on one's own needs, not to think about meeting the needs of another.

This "I deserve" mentality can take us further than we want to go. "I've been under a lot of stress, so I deserve a night out on the town, even though I'm not sure where it will lead." "My spouse has not been as sensitive to my needs as _____. I deserve an affair with someone who really seems to care about me." Pleasure is assumed to be a perk of hard work and success. As Bob Briner notes in *Squeeze Play*, in some cultures a call girl is delivered to your room like a basket of fruit, an expected capstone to a long day's work.

There are a couple of dimensions of the "I deserve" mentality that connect with work. First, the longer you are in a career, the more the "I deserve" mindset settles in. The more seniority, the more perks, the more others should cater to your needs, or the more you excuse your indulgences. Second, if you are overdoing it in your commitment to work, you feel you deserve to overdo it with pleasure as well. When work is extra hard or stressful, you can easily find yourself on the slippery slope of compensation through pleasure.

We all need to do a periodic attitude check—and more than once a year or even more than once a week, maybe even once a day! When an "I deserve" mentality evolves into an "I'll deny myself nothing" approach to life, let the red flags be raised!

APPROACHES TO PLEASURE

The author of Ecclesiastes had access to a plethora of pleasures. His journal contains a whole shopping list of the things he tested: laughter, wine, fulfilling dreams, possessions, greatness, recognition. Here is the list of someone who has "been there" and "done it all." A closer look at his list reveals three approaches to pleasure commonly tried today.

He first tries *overcoming inhibitions*. He adopts the motto posted in the dressing room of comedian Jerry Lewis:

> There are three things that are real: God, human folly, and laughter. Since the first two are beyond our comprehension, we must do what we can with the third.

He wants to laugh, to act foolish. A little wine will help him overcome his inhibitions. He doesn't want to get falling down drunk—just enough to loosen up a little bit.

As already mentioned, I often ask people why they do what they do. When I find out someone spends a lot of time at bars, I try to find out why. Rarely do people go to bars to get smashed, though that may be the end result. Sometimes they go there in search of a relationship, hoping to meet the right lifetime partner or just to arrange a one-night stand. Most often, when I listen closely, I hear that a little alcohol and the bar's atmosphere help them to relax, to unwind, to be who they really are, or to be something they do not normally feel they are.

A few years ago, the TV program *A Current Affair* created a segment on "Hedonism II," a resort in Jamaica.

It billed itself as satisfying every heart's desire. It was a place to really live, to laugh, and to love. One satisfied customer beamed with laughter that he could be a "completely different person" while at the resort. Unrestrained pleasure was justified since "life is too short on this earth, so why not enjoy it?"

Many men believe inhibitions are the by-product of religion. Unfortunately, much of the religion people have experienced leaves them going through motions and wearing masks. They have yet to discover that God created an inhibition-free world and that the cover-up began when God's design was violated (Genesis 2–3). A genuine relationship with God addresses your deepest inhibitions and empowers you to risk "being real" with others.

The second approach of the searcher in Ecclesiastes is *the pleasure of ambition,* that is, to test "what was worthwhile for men to do under heaven." His journal records the ambitious projects he tackled:

- I undertook great projects. (2:4)
- I built houses and planted vineyards. (2:4)
- I made gardens and parks. (2:5)
- I planted all kinds of fruit trees. (2:5)
- I made reservoirs. (2:6)
- I bought slaves. (2:7)
- I owned more. (2:7)
- I amassed more silver and gold. (2:8)
- I acquired singers and a harem. (2:8)
- I became greater. (2:9)

Listen to his action words of accomplishment: *undertook; built; made; planted; bought; owned; amassed; acquired; became.* This man was a doer and a creator.

This section summarizes my personal favorite approach to pleasure. I am not into silliness, although I enjoy a good laugh. I am a bit conservative—my wife uses adjectives like "stodgy" or "boring." While I may never be the life of the party or dance on the tables, I do get a kick out of the adrenaline of accomplishment. There is joy in knowing I have created something.

That can be a healthy approach to pleasure. We have been created in God's image, and he has endowed us as human beings with creative ability and commissioned us to manage his creation (Genesis 1:26–28). We are unique in that we can envision future goals and bring them into being.

This approach, however, has its downside. It is frightening how quickly, yet subtly, the adrenaline of accomplishment becomes the addiction to accomplishment. We have to have that rush of adrenaline to feel that life is fulfilling. We find ourselves saying, "I've done that. What's next?" And what comes next must be bigger and better as our appetite for accomplishment grows. We feel a sense of "success panic" as our to-do list nears completion.

As I write this, our church is constructing a new sanctuary. We had dreamed about it for years, but postponed the dream as we relocated, utilized spartan multipurpose facilities, and prioritized children's educational space. Now the most pressing need is a communication and worship center, and we need to prepare our congregation for a move that will triple our seating capacity. I have been conducting interviews with area churches that have recently constructed new sanctuaries and asking how the transition impacted their "corporate culture"—the congregation's feelings, expectations, and ministry design. I hope to anticipate the changes we will experience.

I have learned plenty, but one observation came through persistently: After the initial exhilaration that comes with the completion of a long-anticipated dream, there was a sense of letdown that impacted nearly everyone.

Really? A sense of letdown after an accomplishment that was dreamed of and carried out, and has eternal consequences?

There is an emptiness that follows the realization of an ambition. We need great ambitions, high ambitions, ambitions worthy of God and of our best effort. But those ambitions also need to be managed. We must control them rather than allow them to control us. Ambition, like all pleasure, makes a great servant but a lousy master.

A third approach to pleasure is found in *making comparisons with others.* I keep one eye on my life, the other eye on someone else's life.

> *I also owned* more *herds and flocks than anyone in Jerusalem before me.* (2:7)
> *I became* greater by far *than anyone in Jerusalem before me.* (2:9)

This approach works great when we are on top of the heap. But how quickly the tables turn when someone edges us out!

You know how it works. You love your big snowblower until your neighbor unveils his bigger snowblower. You love your new car until a coworker purchases the same model with more options. You think your vacation is awesome until someone travels farther and stays longer. You must be selective about the person with whom you compare yourself!

I live in the metropolitan area that is home base for the Amway Corporation. One of the founders, Rich DeVos, is not only a successful entrepreneur and family man, but a tremendous communicator. His inspirational messages challenge thousands of people and touch a variety of dimensions of life. One of the topics he so capably addresses is the tendency of people to live their whole lives through comparisons. By doing so, they never really live their own lives; instead, they are always trying to live someone else's life. That someone sets the agenda for how they live, where they go, and what they buy.

This approach to pleasure connects with the competitive nature of men, but comparison games are played so differently by so many. Some compare only their weaknesses with the strengths of others, and come up short every time. Some choose only people who could never compete with them in a certain area, and so they gloat without reason. Some always compare themselves with the same person—their father, a brother, a friend, or a coworker. Others change the people they compare themselves with every time they pass someone on the way up, or on the way down.

Scripture warns us against this approach to pleasure: "Each one should test his own actions. Then he can take pride in himself, without comparing himself to somebody else" (Galatians 6:4). You can benefit, however, from comparing where you are now to where you were at some point in the past. In this way you will sense the direction your life is heading and the progress you are making.

GRADING THE TEST
(ASSESSMENT OF PLEASURE)

Well, the "pleasure test" has been taken. The Teacher has made a valiant attempt to find the meaning of life in the pursuit of happiness. Like all tests, it is time for the grades to come in. He analyzes the results in two different ways.

First, he does *an immediate assessment.* He asks, "Has the pursuit of pleasure made any difference in my life today?" Here is his conclusion: "My heart took delight in all my work, and this was the reward for all my labor" (2:10). Yes, pleasure added a sense of satisfaction to his life.

He seems to have especially appreciated the realization of his ambitions through hard work; it brought delight and a sense of reward to him.

Pleasure as a reward can provide a strong sense of motivation. Many sales companies motivate their agents or distributors with prizes or vacation opportunities. A friend of mine in the insurance business observes that companies often structure rewards (prizes, trips) so that agents earn them early in their careers. Having once enjoyed that reward, many agents are not satisfied to stop. They want to earn the bigger prize, to win the trip to a more exotic vacation spot.

Sometimes the expectation of pleasure is better than the reality. As one successful businessman in his sixties mused, "The anticipation of a vacation is often better than the real thing. Our imaginations picture the ideal, and we don't live in an ideal world. I have many associates who worked hard for the grand vision of an early retirement. Once the dream became reality, they were restless until they felt they were being productive once again."

Therein lies the paradox in pleasure: The more you seek it, the less you find it. It promises more than it delivers. Happiness is a wonderful by-product of a meaningful life, but it is an elusive goal. The more we focus on it, the harder it becomes to obtain.

One year, through the generosity of a wonderful friend, we were offered a week's stay in an oceanfront condominium in Ft. Lauderdale. Our friend has enjoyed this place for years and said we would enjoy it as well. We loaded our three kids in the car and headed south.

We arrived to find a place more luxurious than we could ever have expected. A doorman was there to greet us and opened the door for us every time we entered and exited (our kids eventually wore him out). We took the semiprivate elevator to our condo—a sprawling floor plan with an ocean view on three sides. Paradise on earth!

Before long we found ourselves alternating between walks on the beach and swimming in the pool. As I sat around the pool, I observed the people who live there most of the year. Perhaps they had sacrificed their whole lives to retire to a place like this. How contented they must be to have their own place in paradise! Not!

I could not help but overhear the conversation of some people sitting near me. There were complaints about the weather, about a local restaurant, and about a nearby store. I subtly moved to another poolside location, feeling my time in "paradise" was being polluted by this complaining. It provided no relief, for again the conversations near me were about petty inconveniences (my perception) that had become major issues (their perception).

Perhaps it was just a bad day around the pool (although the weather was ideal). Or I may have chosen all the wrong lounge chairs. Or the complaining may have been a form of recreation I failed to understand. But it occurred to me that when living in paradise is your only purpose in life, there is a good chance that pettiness will be the by-product.

E. Stanley Jones, in his book *Growing Spiritually*, talks about a fictional person who lives out a fantasy life. All he had to do was think of it and (poof!) it happened. So this man, in a moment of time, sticks his hands in his pockets and leans back and imagines a mansion and (poof!) he has a fifteen-bedroom mansion, three stories with servants instantly available to wait upon his every need.

Why, a place like that needs several fine cars. So he again closes his eyes and imagines the driveway full of the finest wheels money can buy. And (poof!), there are several of the best vehicles instantly brought before his mind's eye. He is free to drive them himself, or sit way back in the limousine with that mafia glass wrapped around the rear, and have the chauffeur drive him wherever he wishes.

There's no place to travel so he comes back home and wishes for a sumptuous meal and (poof!) there's a meal in front of him with all of its mouth-watering aromas and beauty – which he eats alone. And yet ... there was something more he needed to find happiness.

Finally he grows so terribly bored and unchallenged that he whispers to one of the attendants, "I want to get out of this. I want to create some things again. I'd rather be in Hell than be here." To which one of the servants replies quietly, "Where do you think you are?"[1]

Second, perhaps this is why the author of Ecclesiastes reaches a different conclusion in his *ultimate assessment* of pleasure:

> *I thought in my heart, "Come now, I will test you with pleasure to find out what is good." But that also proved to be meaningless.* (2:1)
> *Yet when I surveyed all that my hands had done and what I had toiled to achieve, everything was meaningless, a chasing after the wind; nothing was gained under the sun.* (2:11)

His ultimate assessment? Pleasure is a short-term, time-related feeling, whereas the long-term goal focuses on contentment. The short-term feeling may well be an approach to the long-term goal, but if we focus only on pleasure, we will never experience contentment.

I see this all the time. A successful real estate broker with a pleasure-seeking mentality begins to experiment with cocaine. That experimentation becomes an addiction, and the addiction costs him his career and his credibility as he digs a deep financial hole. Or again, a man begins to notice an attractive coworker. She is naively attentive to him, and he begins to fantasize about an affair with her. A man who for years has carefully built a career, cultivated his marriage and family, and increased his personal net worth trades it all for a moment's pleasure.

Dr. Joseph Stowell has concluded that our society's relentless pursuit of short-term pleasure has created an incredible amount of long-term pain. This is the pleasure/pain fracture of our society. A sexual escapade provides a father with a moment's pleasure but results in excruciating pain for his adolescent children. A materialistic mindset leads a man who finds pleasure by accumulating things to justify it as "providing for his family," while his children live with the pain of never having the one thing from him they want most—his attention.

A few years ago *Atlantic Monthly* contained an article entitled "Dan Quayle Was Right."[2] It reinforced the observation that two-parent families tend to be healthier places for children to grow up than single-parent or stepparent families. It highlighted the impact of family disruptions through divorce. It noted, however, that our society is slow to face the potential negative impact for children. Why? Because this might limit the promise of greater adult choice, freedom, and happiness. We are shifting from a focus on child well-being to adult well-being. Many adults are opting for immediate happiness even though their children will pay for their choices.

The author of Ecclesiastes *focuses on physical and emotional pleasure while shunning the spiritual dimension.*

His search for pleasure was restricted to "under heaven" (2:3) or "under the sun" (2:11). He failed to look "above the sun" for the ultimate answers to the pleasure test. We enjoy "under the sun" pleasures, but we must recognize their limits. Pleasure is a gift from God. Rather than an "I deserve" mentality, we must trust God enough not to have to scramble for pleasure that provides less than the best.

One day I was having breakfast with the mayor of our city, who is committed to "top of the line" living. As he reflected back on his own life and his need to trust God for the best, he recalled his times of service in the Vietnam War. Regularly he received from the States more candy than he could use, and he began to share it with one or two children at the perimeter of his base. Word traveled quickly, and before long a crowd of children gathered to receive candy. The crowd soon grew to a mob. In order to keep the kids from overwhelming him, he would toss handfuls of candy in the air. The kids would scramble frantically to get all that they could.

Of all the kids he saw regularly, two little girls were like "adopted" daughters to him. He wanted them to have the best of the candy. So he instructed them that while the other children scrambled for the candy, they should wait. If they waited, then after the other kids left, these two girls would get the best. They would have to trust him.

When the next opportunity to distribute candy came, he reminded the girls of his promise. The two of them watched anxiously as he tossed handful after handful of candy and the kids scrambled for it. One of the girls could take it no longer–she joined the fray to recover some of the candy. The other girl waited, and just as he promised, he gave her the most and the best.

Pleasure is a gift of God. His best is rarely found in the mad scramble, but in trusting him to provide what is lasting and meaningful. You must overcome the nearly over-whelming feeling of missing out, believing him to provide if you trust him.

For instance, the fantasy that the best fulfillment of sexual desire is beyond marriage is pervasive in our world. Yet in a *U.S. News and World Report* survey, we read a more accurate picture: "Fidelity reigns. ... Married couples have the most sex and enjoy their sex lives more than singles who live alone."[3] That may not sell movie tickets, but it does indicate that God's design of sexual fidelity brings pleasure. Sexual fulfillment and other desires can be managed so that your pleasure is maximized while God's design is honored. Don't pretend your desires for fun, sex, accomplishment, and food do not exist. They are God-given. They can be managed in a way that both pleases you and honors him. Commit yourself to experiencing pleasure as God designed it, not as our world has perverted it.

God is not happy when you are miserable. The test of pleasure provides an opportunity, not to deny our desires, but to develop them, to deepen them, to focus them, and to make the most of them. We learn, like children waiting for candy, that the most and the best are reserved for those who trust God enough to follow his design.

NOTES

1. Chuck Swindoll, *Living on the Ragged Edge* (Waco, Tex.: Word, 1985), p. 48.

2. *Atlantic Monthly* (April, 1993).

3. *U.S. News and World Report* (October 17, 1994).

4

Time Zones of Life

SCRIPTURE: ECCLESIASTES 3:1–17

We are becoming more sophisticated in measuring and managing time. An abundance of seminars and tools promise to help us make the most of time. Our calendars become the records of our lives.

I happen to use the Franklin Planner. I was introduced to it through a seminar. Imagine! A day-long seminar on how to use a calendar! Into that planner go my values, my goals, my priorities, my thoughts, and my notes from meetings and counseling appointments. The leaders of the seminar told me I should never be without my planner–and I rarely am.

One day after leaving the office, I set my planner on top of the car while loading my briefcase into the backseat. I suddenly remembered that I needed to retrieve something from the briefcase, and in the process, I forgot my planner was still on top of the car. I hopped in the car and headed down the road, and as I reached about forty miles an hour, I began to notice sheets of paper flying past the rear window of the car. A sickening feeling came over me as I realized what was happening. It was as if my life was fluttering away!

I pulled off to the side of the busy road. Car after car went by, demolishing the planner and further scattering its pages. Someone noticed my dilemma and graciously stopped to help me retrieve pages from one side of the road while I took the other. I was relieved to recover all but a few pages and was constantly reminded of my mistake over the next few months as I came across pages in my planner with tire tracks on them!

Part of our motivation for managing time comes from its increasing value. Time has been called the "new money." Some futurists project that time will replace money as the dominant indicator of value. A great advantage of money is that it can give you greater control of your time. For example, a person who can afford a car doesn't need to wait for a bus. A profitable business allows its owner to hire employees, thereby freeing himself from some of the time-consuming tasks. The limits of time are greater than the limits of money, which increases the value of time.

With all of your time-management tools, are you doing a better job of investing your time? Or are you simply packing more into an already busy life? Move beyond a "time management" perspective. Discover meaning in life through developing a sense of timing. Learn to discern life's seasons and phases.

EARTH'S TIME ZONE

Over the years I have had a number of opportunities to travel, and in the process have experienced different time zones. A trip to the West Coast means only a few hours difference—a minor adjustment. A trip to Europe or the Middle East represents several hours difference, and the adjustment becomes more difficult. A recent trip I took involved stops in Korea, Singapore, Thailand, Hong Kong, Bangladesh—time zones at least twelve hours different from the one to which I am accustomed. Day becomes night and night becomes day. I stayed long enough to get adjusted to Asian time, then returned home so I could start the adjustment process all over again.

There are two "time zones" in today's journal passage from Ecclesiastes. The first one I have labeled "Earth's time zone": "There is a time for everything, and a season for every activity *under heaven*" (3:1). The author of Ecclesiastes begins his study of life's timing completely apart from God. It is an event-full perspective, a survey of the variety of experiences life offers:

There is a time for everything,
and a season for every activity under heaven:
a time to be born and a time to die,
a time to plant and a time to uproot,
a time to kill and a time to heal,
a time to tear down and a time to build,
a time to weep and a time to laugh,
a time to mourn and a time to dance,
a time to scatter stones and a time to gather them,
a time to embrace and a time to refrain,
a time to search and a time to give up,
a time to keep and a time to throw away,
a time to tear and a time to mend,
a time to be silent and a time to speak,
a time to love and a time to hate,
a time for war and a time for peace. (3:1–8)

The Teacher lists the events of life as a series of contrasts, opposites, or extremes. Many men look at their lives from this point of view. They attempt to pack more and more events into their lives to give life greater meaning. They measure life by events. If they experience happy times, they are happy; if they experience tragic times, they are sad.

But a closer look at the times of life reveals three principles worth noting.

1. Inevitability in Life

Some events in life are beyond our control. Let's take just one contrast from the list: "a time to be born and a time to die" (3:2).

I remember when my wife and I were expecting our first child. I carefully explained to her that she was welcome to give birth any time except Sunday morning. People expected me to communicate truth from God's Word on Sundays. I highlighted the fact that there were six other days in the week, or even Sundays any time after noon was fine. I was sure I had made it clear when would be the most convenient time for us to welcome our firstborn into the world.

So when her water broke 7:00 A.M. Saturday morning, I was proud of her. I thought for sure that we would have this process completed by noon, or at the latest by supper. I could get home at a decent time Saturday evening, look over my notes, and be set to go Sunday morning.

Twenty-eight hours later, around 11:00 A.M. Sunday morning, our son Chris was born. The doctor and I watched Robert Schuller together in the pre-op room while an area pastor took my place at church. In spite of my careful planning, there is "a time to be born."

Some years later, I sat beside the hospital bed of my dying father. He was a great Christian, a man of integrity.

He planned to spend some of his retirement years using his carpentry skills on the mission field. I was overcoming my workaholism, and he was slowing down his business schedule so that we could really spend some quality time together. Now, at just sixty years of age, he was dying. I grudgingly resigned myself to the reality that there is "a time to die."

There are some times of life that are inevitable, circumstances that are beyond our control. My wife reminds me of this every time we are caught in a traffic jam. As I consider switching lanes or navigating the shoulder of the road, she says, "Just relax. There's nothing you can do about it." She's right—though at the time I rarely admit it.

"There's nothing you can do about it." "It's beyond your control." Words like those are not music in the ears of most men. It is not so bad when it refers to a traffic jam that affects a few moments of a day. But what if you suddenly have time on your hands because your company downsized and your supposedly secure job vanished? Or if that downsizing suddenly means mandatory overtime so that work must now consume more hours of your day and more days in your week? That downsizing has a downgrading effect on your family and personal time, and it's beyond your control.

Bob Buford calls these "external conditions"— inevitable happenings over which we have little or no control.[1] From his vantage point, changes in technology revolutionized the television industry, impacting his business. He observes that stubbornness can cause you to expend energy needlessly trying to change something you can only accept. That acceptance can grow until you actually respect the inevitable and begin to find ways creatively to transform those externals into opportunities.

It takes a wise person to distinguish between what you can control (make happen) and what you cannot control (let happen). Many men have experienced burnout trying to change what cannot be changed. That burnout distorts a healthy recognition of what is inevitable into a fatalistic resignation that nothing can be changed. Then you miss life's opportunities.

2. Windows of Opportunity in Life

There is a "season for every activity" (3:1). Pulling another contrast from the Teacher's list, there is "a time to plant and a time to uproot" (3:2). To a farmer, the windows of opportunity are obvious. If he misses the planting season, no matter how much seed he uses or how straight the rows are, he will have no harvest. If he misses the harvest time, ripe fruit becomes rotten and profit becomes loss. For those of us who are not farmers, the windows of opportunity may be less obvious, but they are equally crucial to a "harvest" in life.

Different seasons (opportunities) make different demands on your time. If you are launching a business, you should expect to expend extra time and effort. That will hopefully change as the business matures. In marriage, there are certain windows of opportunity to demonstrate your love. In parenting there are teachable moments that, once missed, may never present themselves again.

One of my heroes is Bill McCartney, former coach of the nationally acclaimed football team from the University of Colorado. He shocked the football world by abruptly resigning from his position as head coach, walking away from a lucrative contract and a successful team. Why? Here is his answer:

"It isn't that I'm burned out on football," McCartney said Thursday. "It's not that I don't enjoy coaching, (because) I do. And I think Colorado football is going to continue to pick up speed.

"It's just that I'm married to a great girl. Today Lyndi and I have been married for 32 years, and we're both healthy. I don't want to just chase the career at the expense of those around me. I've done that long enough. I want to invest more in our marriage while we're still relatively young, and see where that takes us."

McCartney added that he doesn't know what the future holds for him. But he is all but sure of one thing.

"I doubt that I'll coach again," he said. "I just want to do something together, as a team, with my wife. I want to be with her. That's what's in my heart.

"People seem to think there's more to it. There isn't."[2]

In the weeks that followed McCartney's resignation, the national media continued to search for another answer. *Sports Illustrated* devoted several pages to speculation regarding other possible reasons. They could not fathom the courage and priorities it took for a man to look into his wife's face and see a window of opportunity to build more into his marriage.

In order to make the most of opportunities:

- Find them in the moments of a day. *The Wall Street Journal,* in an article on the increasing length of the average commute to work, interviewed many people who were using this "wasted" time to do their best thinking, to listen to life-enriching tapes, or to grab some necessary downtime as they adjust between environments.[3]
- Find them in the seasons of life. Jim Buick, former CEO of the Zondervan Corporation, shared his future plans with a group of business and professional persons. Some were asking if, at sixty years of age, he planned to head another company. He replied, "Generals tend to go to battle in the spring." It was his way of saying he likely would not lead another business. He was excited, though, about the opportunity of consulting with business-persons who could benefit from his experience.
- Realize you cannot seize every opportunity. Sometimes two "windows" open at the same time. A friend of mine with young children had an opportunity to buy into a business. His family and his demanding business led him to scale back other commitments. He was struggling with these cutbacks until he had lunch with Max DePree. Max, who benefits so many organizations through his board involvement, revealed that when his children were young and his responsibilities at Herman Miller were more demanding, he served on only one board. In reality, the demands of one or two opportunities limit your pursuits in other areas.

- Recognize that shifting from one opportunity to another can be uncomfortable. A man who invests tremendous time and energy into initiating a business may feel a bit guilty when he no longer invests as much effort at work, even though he knows it is not necessary. This discomfort can cause you to miss new opportunities as you make unreasonable investments in old ones.

3. Time for the Various Responsibilities of Life

Each obligation you have in life carries with it certain demands on your time. The ability to assess accurately the time necessary to fulfill various responsibilities is part of the "burden" of a well-managed life. "What does the worker gain from his toil? I have seen the burden God has laid on men" (3:9–10). The responsibility that probably makes the most demands on your time is your career.

I have had a wonderful relationship with the governing board of our church since we began our congregation in 1979. Suppose I were to announce to them one day: "I love being your pastor, and I hope to serve with you for years to come. I do not, however, want to work any more on the weekends or on holidays." I can hear their response: "We wish you well in your new place of ministry!"

Serving as a pastor means showing up on weekends. Many people may wonder what I do between weekends, but when our Saturday night and Sunday services roll around, they expect me to be there most of the time. While Christmas Eve may be a relaxed family time for most, it is an opportunity for our church to communicate God's love and truth to thousands of people in multiple services throughout the evening. For me, working weekends and holidays is part of my career commitment.

Let's face it, though. There is a tendency for men to *overestimate* the time necessary to fulfill work responsibilities. Bill McCartney, the Colorado coach mentioned earlier, says he and his coaches tended to "overprepare" for games, spending more time than was really necessary, to the neglect of other responsibilities.

This overcommitment has a downside. More businesses than ever recognize that the quality, not the quantity, of the hours makes the difference. As Gilbert Fuchsberg warns, "If you consistently labor long hours, you risk upstaging your boss, being tainted as inefficient and receiving unwanted extra assignments."[4] He observes that education, experience, productivity, and responsiveness to clients' perceptions tend to matter more. Some companies are even beginning to teach their employees the importance of a balanced life!

A more serious downside in overcommitment to work is its impact on relationships. It has been captured in one way in the turn-of-the-century Yiddish song, "Mayn Yingele" ("My Little One"), which a father sings to his sleeping child:

I have a son, a little son,
A boy completely fine.
When I see him it seems to me
That all the world is mine.

But seldom, seldom do I see
My child awake and bright;
I only see him when he sleeps;
I'm only home at night.

It's early when I leave for work;
When I return it's late.
Unknown to me is my own flesh,
Unknown is my child's face.

When I come home so wearily
In the darkness after day,
My pale wife exclaims to me:
"You should have seen our child play."

I stand beside his little bed,
I look and try to hear.
In his dreams he moves his lips:
"Why isn't Papa here?"⁵

This song was written in 1897 when Papa and Mama put long hours in at the sweatshop. Those days may be gone, but the long hours for many remain.

There is a double whammy here. While overestimating the time a career requires, men tend to *underestimate* the time that being a husband and father requires. It was not so dangerous a century ago when a farmer worked seventy hours a week since his family was working right along with him. But as our work worlds have distanced us from our home life, the danger of overcommitment to work and undercommitment to family has distanced us from the people we love most. The average man would be better off spending a little less time (than he thinks is necessary) on his career and a little more time (than he thinks is necessary) with his family.

This means you should be as intentional and accountable regarding time for family as you are regarding time for work. For instance, in 1994, when my oldest child turned thirteen, we had a special "blessing" time for him that involved some of our closest friends. I then offered to him what has since become known as "teen time"–a time at least once every two weeks for him and me to be alone together. I limit the amount of money we spend during teen time (so that it is not just a matter of spending money to have a good time) and try to maximize time in settings where we can talk. I am accountable to him (and to my accountability partner) for this "teen time."

Accountability for allotting time to fulfill all of your responsibilities keeps you from self-deception. If you want something bad enough, there is a strong tendency to minimize the time required and rationalize away any objections that might be raised.

On the foundational level, it is a matter of trust—trusting God. Do you seek to honor God, living with integrity and working productively? Then you should be able to say no to additional responsibilities that overload time commitments. You can set limits on your hours while you seek to be the best employee possible, trusting God to open up the career path he knows is best for you. That requires adjustment to another time zone—eternity's time zone.

ETERNITY'S TIME ZONE

After reviewing the variety of times and seasons that make up life, the journal of Ecclesiastes records a transition from a purely "eventful" perspective to an eternal perspective. After focusing on what happens "under heaven," God becomes included in the picture. How does he get involved in the timing of our lives? How does heaven touch earth, causing his timing and a person's timing to intersect?

1. Recognizing the Beauty God Brings to Life

From earth's time zone, many of life's events seem inevitable. Life's ups and downs elude your ability to control them. God's beauty has a way of redeeming the inevitability in life:

He has made everything beautiful in its time.
He has also set eternity in the hearts of men; yet
they cannot fathom what God has done from
beginning to end. (3:11)

God has made everything beautiful in its time. Another word for "beautiful" is "appropriate." God is in control, causing whatever happens to fit his purposes for your life.

Frankly, I wish God would adjust to my timetable. Try as I might to change it, he has his own schedule, and it often does not parallel mine. If you truly want to discover God's will for your life, you face two equally difficult challenges:

- Knowing *what* God wants – the *content* of his plan for you. What does he want you to be and to do? How does he want you to act?
- Knowing *when* God wants something to happen – the *calendar* of his plan for you. When does he want you to act?

The more discrepancy there is between his time frame and your time frame, the greater the requirement for trust. This is the "timing and trust" hurdle.

If you pray for a new career opportunity and ask God to provide it within six months, as long as God meets your expectations, it requires little trust. But when six months have gone by, every additional day that passes requires a little more trust. The "trust" test begins when your time expectations are not met. Suppose you want your wife to see things your way in a particular area within one week. Even if it is God's will to change her mind (for some reason, he usually chooses to change you!), after a week has passed, you must begin to trust God's timing as best.

God answers prayer in various ways:

1. Yes: God gives you what you want, when you want it.
2. No: God's will is different, and he will not give you what you have asked for.
3. Later: What you want is fine, it is just not "appropriate" (beautiful) right now.

It is that last answer that throws off your timing. But God's "beauty" is often created in you or in your circumstances as you adjust to his timing.

You can sense God's timing because he has "set eternity in the hearts of men" (3:11). You are a unique creation of God. You can be aware of the "transcendent," that which is beyond your natural senses:

- You can envision the future, bringing hope when things are not unfolding as planned.
- You can envision the future, rising above the patterns of life (which seem inevitable and are beyond our control) to the potential of life (which God makes beautiful under his control).

"Eternity in the hearts of men" helps you develop a vision for life that transcends the seasons of life. As philosopher William James wrote: "The great use of life is to spend it for something that will outlast it." That's sensing eternity.

There is a reality check, however. "Yet they cannot fathom what God has done from beginning to end" (3:11). You are not going to figure everything out, or else you would be in control instead of God. There will always be the element of mystery. You will not fathom it all, but God graciously gives you glimpses to build your trust in his timing.

2. Never Taking God's Generosity for Granted

Meaning is pressed into life as we recognize every moment and every activity as a gift from God:

> *I know that there is nothing better for men than to be happy and do good while they live. That everyone may eat and drink, and find satisfaction in all his toil—this is the gift of God.* (3:12–13)

The Teacher lists five gifts from God here: to be happy, to do good, to eat, to drink, and to find satisfaction in work.

When everyday opportunities are perceived as gifts from God, you can enjoy even the simplest of things—a good meal, a refreshing drink, a good day's work. In contrast, if you have an "I deserve" mentality (I deserve something more, I deserve something different), nothing quite satisfies.

When each day is a gift, you can enjoy today. Unfortunately, many men live for the day they will receive a promotion. Single men live for the day they will be married. Married men live for the day they will have children. Those who have children live for the day when children leave home! Workers live for the day they will retire. But retirement fails to meet their expectations. Why? They have postponed enjoyment of a lifetime's worth of gifts to a few years at its end.

Recently I shared these thoughts with a friend. The "light came on" for him. He had a successful career, a decent salary, opportunity to travel, and meaningful times with family. Yet the company he worked for had proposed a restructuring that would substantially improve his position, both financially and professionally. He found himself living for that day and fretted about anything that delayed its arrival. As we talked, he began to realize life was passing him by because of a focus on what he "deserved" and when he might get it. He responded with a commitment to enjoy each day, in his present circumstances, as a gift of God.

3. Remembering Your Accountability to God

It is disheartening to see men who squander the opportunities of life prosper, or to see men who carefully pursue the opportunities of life encounter failure. Some use "smoke and mirrors" to create an image of productivity at work and receive promotions, while others with exemplary work ethics are passed over.

The author of Ecclesiastes wants us to know the ultimate scorecard is found in the hands of God.

I thought in my heart,
"God will bring to judgment
both the righteous and the wicked,
for there will be a time for every activity,
a time for every deed." (3:17)

This means that if you are fooling everybody, including yourself, while neglecting to spend proper time pursuing the commitments you espouse, God is not fooled. It also means that if you devote time to properly fulfill your responsibilities, but the rewards are few and the applause nonexistent, God will set the record straight someday.

Since God keeps a perfect record of time, "top of the line" living means recognizing your accountability to him. Seek to be a good manager of life's opportunities. Learn to pursue agendas and schedules that reflect his purposes. Discover his "calling" for your life in the arenas of family, career, and personal well-being. Sense eternity's time zone.

My Franklin Planner contains a quote from Benjamin Franklin:

> To Love Life Is To Love Time.
> Time Is The Stuff Life Is Made Of.

Peter Drucker makes us aware that "time is the scarcest resource, and until it is managed, nothing else can be managed." "Top of the line" time management is more than clocks and calendars. Many men use those tools to pack more into their schedules, becoming busier and busier while their lives become emptier and emptier. The following action steps will give you a greater sense of timing in life.

1. *Present your schedule to God.* Open your calendar and ask God what his purpose might be for your activity in each day. You have your agenda, but be consciously aware that God might have something else in mind for that lunch appointment or that time with your child, something you have not yet considered:

> *Teach us to number our days aright, that we may gain a heart of wisdom.* (Moses in Psalm 90:12)
> *Show me, O LORD, my life's end and the number of my days; let me know how fleeting is my life.* (David in Psalm 39:4)
> *Be very careful, then, how you live—not as unwise but as wise, making the most of every opportunity, because the days are evil.* (Paul in Ephesians 5:15–16)

Moses, King David, the apostle Paul—they presented their schedules to God. A moment's honesty and humility before God and your calendar each day will gradually enhance the significance of every activity.

2. *Monitor your attitude for gratitude.* God wants you to enjoy him and to enjoy life. Not someday, but today!

While you anticipate future opportunities, live with contentment today. Do not miss God's gifts that are often wrapped in the plainest and simplest of packages. Each day identify at least one thing in your life that you are grateful for, and then tell someone.

3. *Invest your time in what lasts.* People last for eternity, so they merit prime time. Likewise God's purposes are lasting:

> *I know that everything God does will endure forever; nothing can be added to it and nothing can be taken from it. God does it so that men will revere him.* (3:14)

That means that the more you align your priorities with God's purposes, the more lasting will be the results of your life. Do not try to twist God's arm to bless what you are doing, but seek to discover what he blesses. Then commit yourself to do it.

The first house my wife and I owned was located around the corner from a Chicken Coop restaurant. Wanting to provide my wife with a wonderful dining experience (and having already made numerous visits to Wendy's), we decided to eat at that Chicken Coop one noon. We ordered our meal, sat down in the booth, and then noticed an unexpected quote on the paper products of this fast-food restaurant:

Only one life, 'twill soon be past;
Only what's done for Christ will last.

Somewhere along the line this restaurant owner had linked fried chicken to a sense of God's calling on his life! Aligning your activities with God's intentions does not mean spending all of your time at church, reading the Bible, or praying. It does, however, mean your church attendance, Bible reading, and prayer times link your schedule with God's will.

You and I will never experience eternity's time zone and true effectiveness in the middle of frantic activity. Busyness robs you of more than relaxation; it robs you of an awareness of God's timing. God's attempts to get through to you are often met with a busy signal—not only the busyness around you, but also the busyness within you.

It is popular to be busy. Many people start their conversations with me by saying, "I know you're busy, but. ..." Not, "Hi, how are you?" or "How have you been?" Just, "I know you're busy, but. ..." How do you respond to an opening like that? If I say "No, I'm not that busy," they think I am either lying or lazy. If I say "I sure am," it may indicate I am disorganized or disinterested in hearing what they say. So I have developed this standard response, "Yes, I'm busy, but comfortably so." I invite you to be "comfortably busy"—comfortable that you are living with calmness of spirit and yet investing your life in ways that have meaning. It's a matter of timing.

NOTES

1. Bob Buford, *Half Time* (Grand Rapids: Zondervan, 1995), p. 154.

2. *The Grand Rapids Press* (December 31, 1994).

3. Kathleen Deveny and Gabriella Stern, "Another Day, Another Three-Hour Commute, *The Wall Street Journal* (December 2, 1994), p. B1.

4. *The Wall Street Journal* (July 27, 1994).

5. *The Wall Street Journal* (December 29, 1994).

5

Acquaintances 93, Friends 0

SCRIPTURE: ECCLESIASTES 4:9–12

Maybe a traumatic experience served as a wake-up call. I remember gathering with some men one morning to talk about relationships. One of the guys shared that not long after moving to our community, his wife's car was hit by a drunk driver. As he sat in the hospital emergency room in the middle of the night, not knowing if his wife would live or die, he wondered whom he should call. His aloneness was overwhelming. As his mind came up empty on names, his heart was haunted by the realization that he had a hundred acquaintances, but no one to call—no real friends who could share this dark moment with him.

Others in the group, including myself, were touched by his story, not only because of our concern for him, but because we knew his feelings. Men have lots of acquaintances. Sometimes we even call them friends. But, to borrow the *Ghostbusters* phrase—"Who ya gonna call?"

It may not be a traumatic experience that gets our attention. But sooner or later we begin to recognize our tendency as men to expend so much energy generating functional success in our careers that we realize we have not taken the time to consider relational success. Many men then try easy but costly substitutes to numb the pain of loneliness:

- Frequenting bars, which offer a stimulating but superficial environment
- Becoming entangled in an adulterous relationship because of feeling lonely and uncared for in a marriage
- Responding to peer pressure to experiment with drugs or overindulge in alcohol
- "Hiring" relationships with counselors or consultants, not motivated by personal or professional growth but by a desire to get someone to care
- Lowering ethical standards in business out of the fear of rejection that might come with losing an account
- Tragically taking one's life, believing that no one cares

In our society and as men, passive allegiance will never lead to meaningful friendships. You will have to swim upstream in a world where people are losing connection and families are falling apart. You must invest in relationships, standing apart from the throngs of lost and rootless men who drift through life without a sense of belonging or of allegiance to anything. Our world is changing; progress often comes at the expense of relationships. Where will the currents of change take your relationships if you fail to act?

ARENAS OF ACQUAINTANCE

According to the author of Ecclesiastes, "Two are better than one, because they have a good return for their work" (4:9). He highlights in this section some of the arenas in which relationships get their start.

Some acquaintances are situational, or what I would call *activity-based*. These relationships are based on a common activity, such as working together or recreation together. You get to know a person because you belong to the same club or work in the same department. Your kids play soccer together, so for ten consecutive Saturday mornings you stand along the sidelines talking about kids, soccer, the weather, or the latest headlines.

You can tell a relationship is activity-based because when the activity goes away, the relationship goes away. Someone switches departments, so you no longer see each other. Soccer season ends and you may never connect again, unless your kids are on the same team next year.

Other acquaintances form because individuals are fighting a common enemy or facing a common struggle: "If one falls down, his friend can help him up. But pity the man who falls and has no one to help him up" (4:10). Such relationships are *recovery-based*. People are supportive of each other as they work through the stages of restoration to wholeness. Earlier this century Bill Wilson demonstrated that alcoholics could regain sobriety in a twelve-step process. Those steps have been the foundation of a burgeoning recovery movement addressing the woes of overeating, sexual addiction, and other common struggles. Individual effort is augmented with small support groups, and the buddy system provides reality checks and reinforces willpower. Relationships that are recovery-based often fade as the person gains small victories and rebuilds his life.

Other relationships grow out of a common commitment. They are *loyalty-based*, arising out of shared needs or goals:

Also, if two lie down together, they will keep warm.
  But how can one keep warm alone?
Though one may be overpowered,
  two can defend themselves.
A cord of three strands is not quickly broken. (4:11–12)

This loyalty is seen in families, whether they are functional or dysfunctional. Such loyalties may have been nurtured by a common history or may be reinforced by a common vision for the future. The commitment may be to marriage (for better, for worse; for richer, for poorer . . .), providing a foundation for oneness between husband and wife. The commitment may be to Christ and a common church family or to a common ministry cause.

    With these relationships, a change in loyalties brings a change in relationship. For example, if one member of the family makes a commitment to Christ while another does not, this creates an uneasy feeling of being unequally yoked. A similar feeling may arise when someone once registered as a Democrat decides to become a Republican.

    Activity, recovery, loyalty—these are natural arenas where networking occurs and acquaintances form. In these connections the potential is present for some real friendships.

THE RELATIONSHIP SCORE

    Acquaintances add meaning to life. I celebrate the variety of people with whom my life intersects, even if it is a one-time event. My concern lies in the relationship "score" of many men:

Acquaintances–93, Friendships–0

There is nothing inappropriate about having 93, or even hundreds, of acquaintances. But there is no way a person can have 93 close friends. The question is, "Do you have

one acquaintance that is developing into true friendship?"
Do you have two friends? three friends? Why do most men
have so many acquaintances and no real friends?

1. Pace of Life

Richard Swenson is a medical doctor who encourages
people to build "margin" into their lives.[1] He argues that
the fullness of life is found by living in all "four gears":

- Overdrive: the gear we use when our
  responsibilities demand extra hours or energy
- Drive: the gear in which we are normally active–
  our daily work and recreation
- Low: the gear in which we form relationships with
  other people
- Park: the gear in which we survey our soul and
  develop a relationship with God ("Be still, and
  know that I am God").

Our busy society requires higher revving engines, so many
men never slow down enough (externally or internally) to
form deep relationships with God or with others. You can
form acquaintances as you dash from one demand to
another, but it is impossible to go below the surface with a
"rush hour" lifestyle. No one can develop deep friendships
on the run.

2. Transience of Society

Several years ago an associate pastor from our church
near Grand Rapids, Michigan, went to plant a new church
in a northeast suburb of Atlanta, Georgia. He had lived in
that area of Atlanta during his teen years and developed a
vision for reaching that community. However, he found it
extremely difficult to get beyond polite interaction with the

people he met. Being a people person and skilled in forming relationships, he took people's reactions to him a bit personally. He thought the reserved response was due to his being a "northerner" moving into a southern community, but the majority of people he encountered were transplanted northerners themselves!

So he did a bit more investigating and discovered that many of his acquaintances worked for large corporations. They planned on living in the Atlanta area for two or three years before being transferred to continue their climb up the corporate ladder. Knowing they would be moving, they avoided forming close friendships to minimize the pain of separation. As a result, they "cocooned" within their homes, keeping neighbors and coworkers at an amiable arm's length.

A man in our community has had a similar experience in a somewhat different way. He plans to live in his present house for years to come, so he wants to become an integrated part of the community. But so many of his neighbors have moved in a relatively brief time that he and his wife feel hesitant to form friendships with them.

This hesitation caused by our highly mobile society, combined with life in high gear, creates a one-two punch against deep friendships. The conditions of contemporary life have leeched out the ingredients of community once so prevalent. Years ago in farming communities, people lived their whole lives on one piece of property, perhaps inherited from their parents, and *had* to work together as a community to build barns and harvest crops. Communities were much more friendship-friendly.

The mobility factor in our culture relates not only to work but also to recreation. Scores of people live in the north part of the year and in the south during the winter months. Others have lake property that is their home from

Memorial Day to Labor Day. They hesitate to invest themselves to any extent in churches or community organizations
because, as they say, "We'll be gone from x month to x
month." They have acquaintances in each of their living
locations but hesitate to form friendships because, "We'll
soon be heading back."

3. Distractions of Technology

In earlier times when families gathered at home or
friends came over, you had to talk to each other. There
were no options! Now, however, you can listen to your
stereos (with headphones!), use your fax and phone (even
from your car), choose from hundreds of different cable TV
channels, pick up a video for the VCR, or play video games.

By the time a typical American school child graduates
from high school, he or she will have spent 11,000 hours in
school and 15,000 hours in front of the television tube. A
Michigan State University study cites the results of a group
of four- and five-year-olds who were asked to choose
between giving up television or giving up their fathers.
One-third said they would give up Dad! *The Wall Street
Journal* may provide part of the reason; it notes that moms
and dads are depicted as the scariest monsters on any
screen. Frazzled, overworked, or neglectful working parents
are an emerging stereotype in family TV and movies, and
the message is mostly negative.[2]

Entertainment can be an easy substitute for the hard
work of building friendships. Watching a conversation on
the screen is easier than having one in the home. A week-
long "fast" from television or taking the phone off the hook
is a good first step for families or friends wanting to take
their relationship to a deeper level.

4. Changing Roles

Men, our roles are changing. We are not only expected to be breadwinners, but be sensitive as well! *Newsweek* recently asked, "Now who gets the blame—and the credit—for social ills and cures? Dear old Dad."[3] The absence of fathers physically and emotionally from their families has become a national issue since Dan Quayle's 1992 reference to Murphy Brown in a lecture on parenthood. Fatherhood is now not only a sacred trust but a public-policy agenda item. *Faith Today* carried a cover story on "Reinventing Dad."[4] *The Wall Street Journal* discussed men at war, as the sensitive 1990s-type square off against the old-fashioned "regular" guys, and everybody feels the strain.[5]

That strain has led many men to avoid relationships rather than attempt to adjust to evolving expectations. In relationships we feel out of control. As one man told me, "At the office and country club I get respect. People actually think I have good ideas! Do you know the last time my teenage kids gave me that impression? I find myself escaping to the office or country club. The confidence coming from clearly defined roles is replaced with uncertainty."

5. Lack of Commitment

Of all the reasons for the relationship score (Acquaintances 93, Friends 0), I am convinced that the primary issue is lack of commitment. Acquaintances are valuable, tend to form quickly, and are a matter of convenience. Friendships are indispensable, tend to form gradually, and are a matter of commitment. Acquaintances are a starting point, friendship is the goal to be sought.

This lack of commitment is evident in even the deepest of relationships. People enter marriage with a consumer mentality, looking for a partner who can supply their needs. Family life is valued as long as it does not hinder a man from pursuing his varied individual interests. Relationships, even marriage, are pictured by the media as having utilitarian purposes (preventing juvenile delinquency, raising test scores for children in school, etc.) but not having an ultimate purpose in and of themselves. Relationships are a means, not an end.

It will take real commitment to deepen your acquaintances into friendship. There may be shortcuts to acquaintances (developing certain hobbies or joining organizations), but there are no shortcuts to friendship. If you want a friend, you must make a commitment to be a friend.

FORMING FRIENDSHIPS

What are the commitments that, over time, form friendships? Let's go back to the words of the man who first concluded that "two are better than one, because they have a good return for their work" (4:9). That is, you can accomplish more by working cooperatively than by working individually.

I am told that if you place one of those magnificent draft horses in a harness, alone it can pull up to two tons of weight. How much weight could two draft horses, hitched together, pull? While you might logically conclude four tons, the answer is up to twenty-three tons. Two are better than one!

Workers, of course, are not draft horses, but corporations are recognizing the value of teamwork. Cooperating with others maximizes strengths. Weaknesses are minimized as the strength of one person makes the weakness of another irrelevant. A "task force with a singular focus" is replacing the "standing committee" to give organizations greater flexibility.

I believe the first foundation for effectiveness in friendship, not just productivity, is a *commitment to co-operation.* We all know the value of cooperation—who could argue against it? It is like motherhood or apple pie, a value nearly everyone espouses. That is probably why I was surprised a few years back when a consultant came in to administer a stress test to our church staff. It indicated I live a rather stress-free life (someone commented that was due to the fact I tend to create stress for others rather than feel it myself!), but there were a couple of areas of concern. One was that "cooperating with others" was a source of stress for me.

I immediately assumed the test was wrong—that conclusion is always more comfortable than facing reality! After all, our church over the years has fulfilled its vision through strong teamwork among the pastoral staff and throughout the congregation. The Bible itself has set the standard for cooperation by calling the church the body of Christ—the eye needs the hand, and the head needs the foot (1 Corinthians 12:21). We cannot function without each other.

So what was the issue? The feedback I received made it painfully obvious: Cooperation involves trust, letting go, and relinquishing control. By nature I value cooperation as long as things are still done how I want and when I want. I have to learn what is unnatural to me, that is, taking the risk involved in trusting others. It can be diagrammed this way:

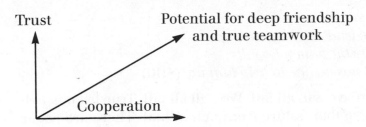

This commitment to cooperation goes against the grain of acceptable egocentrism in relationships. This egocentrism says, "I shouldn't have to make adjustments in order to have a relationship with you. If a relationship just happens, that's fine. If not, then it must be that our lifestyles are incompatible to forming a friendship with each other." The aversion to lifestyle-altering cooperation keeps acquaintances multiplying but friendships aborting before they can form.

Recently a man in our church bought into a business. He was repeatedly warned against forming a partnership, even though both men were Christians and had similar values. The reasons he was given included, "You won't have complete control"; "You will have to make adjustments that you won't necessarily like"; and "You won't have total decision-making authority." While partnerships have their drawbacks, why do Christian advisors assume shared ownership and the necessity for cooperation are negative qualities?

Acquaintances allow you to be in control. Friendships require that you risk trusting instead of competing. Friends recognize that they need each other. There is a sense of belonging to each other, a sense of mutual responsibility to make the friendship work.

Added to the commitment to cooperation is a *commitment to restoration*:

If one falls down,
  his friend can help him up.
But pity the man who falls
  and has no one to help him up! (4:10)

As men, we will all fail. We will all fall. True friends help you keep that failure from being final. There are eagles who love to soar with you on the winds of success but who quickly become vultures, picking at you when you encounter the downdraft of failure. Friendship is the hand that helps you up when you have fallen, not the foot in the back that keeps you facedown in failure.

Among your acquaintances there are "good-time" relationships, the people who relate to your success. They will be around as long as you are on a roll. Among your acquaintances there are also "bad-time" relationships, the people who relate to your struggle. While they may be a bit intimidated by your successes, your failures help them feel good about themselves, and they will be around during the valleys of life. One would hope that among your acquaintances will also be a few "all-time" friends. They will rejoice with us when we rejoice and mourn with us when we mourn (see Romans 12:15).

Who will be there when you fail? Who is the man, or men, who will help you up when you fall? That is a true indicator of who your real friends are.

Jackie Robinson was the first black man to play major league baseball. In the early days of his illustrious career, he faced hostile crowds in every stadium. One day while playing at his home park in Brooklyn, he made an error. The Dodger fans began to boo Jackie mercilessly. He just stood there, devastated, while the fans kept on yelling insults at him. Then shortstop Pee Wee Reese ran over and put his arm around Jackie's shoulder. The curious fans stopped their shouting. They stared at the two men standing together. Jackie later confided that he was not sure whether he would have continued his career had it not been for that arm around his shoulder. When a friend fails, will you be a fan booing from the stands or a Pee Wee Reese by his side?

There are times when a man experiences "circumstantial" failure–an error on the ball diamond, a poor investment, or a misjudgment of a person's abilities. Often circumstantial failure involves dimensions beyond his control. Certainly this is a test of friendship.

At other times a man experiences "character" failures. Character decisions are within his control, but he makes the wrong choices. Then the spirit within him falls apart. This failure goes deeper and strikes at the core of who a man is. This is an even greater test of friendship.

The commitment to help a fallen friend may involve confronting, or "care-fronting." "Care-fronting" says, "I care enough about you to be up-front with you." It is more than pointing out a problem, although that may be a necessary step in breaking through the denial that often accompanies failure. It involves lifting the other person up and encouraging him as you stand side by side to face the failure and rebuild life.

A third commitment necessary to forming friendship is aligned with the two already mentioned, but the way the author of Ecclesiastes phrases it is a bit unusual:

Also, if two lie down together, they will keep warm.
  But how can one keep warm alone? (4:11)

This kind of snuggling to keep warm may have once been necessary, but how does it apply in a day when we can adjust the temperature on our waterbeds or electric blankets? It may be best applied today as a "word picture," not just of physical warmth, but *warmth in relationships*– the warmth that keeps our hearts from growing cold. It is the warmhearted feeling that comes when people share their lives openly and honestly with one another. We have all felt the difference between being given the cold shoulder and receiving a warm welcome.

Some marriages are cold, amounting to little more than peaceful coexistence. Other marriages are intimate, deep and heartwarming. Some parent-child relationships resemble a cease-fire agreement in a war zone. Other parents have a mutually nurturing and fulfilling relationship with their children. There are churches that leave us cold, while other churches exude an atmosphere of love and acceptance.

For many men the idea of warmth and affirmation in a friendship is hard to grasp. We are conditioned by society or family to be private and performance-oriented, to the point that sharing feelings and love is perceived as weakness. This may even be true in one of the most important relationships in a man's life–his marriage. A businessman with whom I am acquainted was motivated to seek a counselor to help "warm up" his communication with his wife. The psychologist recommended the following conversation as a guideline to greater understanding and warmth in dealing with a concern or problem in the relationship:

1. What did you *feel* (emotionally)?
2. Could you explain why you were feeling this? Summarize: What I hear you saying is _____
3. What do you *need* from me?
4. Could you *explain* why this is important to you?

This man, even though skilled in acquaintance-making, said this process at first felt unnatural and mechanical. As he became more comfortable, along with his wife, in having this conversation, it enhanced the affirmation of each other's feelings. He learned to affirm.

Affirmation is something most of us need to learn to give consistently. I am trying to learn this skill in building my relationship with my teenage son, who, like his dad, is strong-willed. If I challenge him will to will, we grow distant. If I go for his heart and share my heart, we draw closer.

Relationships breathe, fluctuating between closeness and distance. It is in closeness that a relationship develops intimacy; it is in distance that each individual develops identity. Sometimes people are affirming when they feel close to another person and critical when they feel a distance. A commitment to affirmation, however, means sharing my heart with you as well as giving you the space you need to continue growing as a person.

A final commitment in forming friendship is *mutual protection*:

Though one may be overpowered,
  two can defend themselves.
A cord of three strands is not quickly broken. (4:12)

There is greater security and protection through unity. This is true in battle, whether fighting side-by-side or back-to-back. It reduces our blind spots when we are watching out for each other. Rarely will physical protection be necessary, but there are plenty of emotional and spiritual battles where going it alone leaves us in a vulnerable position.

Bob Briner, in his book *Squeeze Play*, shares practical insights for men caught between work and home. By his own estimation his business travels have meant spending over a thousand nights in hotel rooms all over the world. He believes that next to sexual temptation, loneliness is the weapon of choice used against Christian men in the 1990s. The despair of loneliness and the false promise of illicit sexual delight are a powerful one-two punch aimed squarely at vulnerable men, and knockouts are scored far too frequently.[6]

True friendship creates protection through positive peer pressure to make right choices and set proper priorities. It provides a safety net for those times when we do not know our own hearts. We can easily develop weaknesses, excuse quirks in our personality, or neglect areas of needed growth without someone to help us identify the blind spots that we fail to see in ourselves.

One of my desires is to serve the church where I am now pastor for a long time – maybe a lifetime. The vision God has given to me and to our church will take many years to become reality. Some years ago an experienced pastor gave me this input when I asked him for the keys to effective long-term pastorates. First, he mentioned the importance of personal growth, professionally and spiritually. As he put it, "A growing church needs a growing leader." But I will never forget his second piece of advice: "Don't do anything stupid." He went on to say that many men, in a vulnerable moment, have done something stupid that compromised their credibility and integrity. That thing may have cost him his job, his marriage, and his future. A friend or two keeps us alert to pitfalls we might otherwise not see.

The commitments of friendship require us to face four common fears:

Commitment	*Fear*
1. Cooperation to have a good return for work	1. That I will not accomplish anything worthwhile in life
2. Restoration to help a person who has fallen	2. That my failure will be final
3. Affirmation of who I am and what I feel	3. That I will be lonely
4. Protection in the middle battles	4. That I am vulnerable and will not persevere

If our fears often rob us of a meaningful life, our friend-ships release the opportunity for meaning in life.

SUGGESTIONS FOR "TOP OF THE LINE" FRIENDSHIPS

1. Recognize that acquaintances are valuable and should be cultivated. Recognize also that there is a level of relationship beyond acquaintances and that you will never experience it without intentional effort.

2. Be willing to risk trusting another person, even if that person does not always do things as you like. Be willing to reduce your need to control.

3. It takes a real man to share his feelings. Words like love, kindness, compassion, and tenderness are not feminine adjectives. They were used to describe the greatest man who ever lived—Jesus Christ. Begin to think of yourself in these terms and act accordingly.

4. Locate one or two men who can provide some accountability for you. Share your goals and priorities and extend the freedom for him to ask the tough questions.

5. Welcome the challenges that deep relationships will undoubtedly bring to your life. As an individual, God develops his character in you only to a certain point. His next work in you is done in the context of relationship. God is the one who created you and first concluded that "it is not good for the man to be alone" (Genesis 2:18). For instance, many people who enter marriage are not nearly as shocked by the discovery of what their partner is really like as they are with the discovery of what they themselves are really like! It is a bit disconcerting to see your children turn out like you. God places you in relationships like marriage, parenting, and true friendship to continue his work in you.

6. Be willing to *learn* to be a friend. A few years ago it dawned on me that I had hundreds of acquaintances but had failed to invest my life in ways that would develop a few good friends. More than that, I was not even sure I knew how to be a friend. I approached a couple guys I respected and said:

> I'd like to be your friend. I'm not sure I know how to be a friend. I feel like I'm in kindergarten when it comes to my knowledge of deep friendship. But I would like to learn, and I would like to become your friend.

I have learned a lot in the years since those conversations first took place. I am all the way up to the middle of first grade when it comes to friendship! It is sometimes humbling, sometimes exhilarating, but always worth it, because:

Two are better than one.

NOTES

1. Richard A. Swenson, *Margin* (Colorado Springs, Colo.: NavPress, 1992).

2. *The Wall Street Journal* (October 26, 1994).

3. *Newsweek* (October 31, 1994).

4. *Faith Today* (September/October 1994).

5. *The Wall Street Journal* (June 21, 1993).

6. Bob Briner, *Squeeze Play* (Grand Rapids: Zondervan, 1994), p. 15.

6

Promises Are Made
to Be ... Kept

SCRIPTURE: ECCLESIASTES 5:1–7

Linda Wertheimer is one of many thought-provoking personalities regularly heard on National Public Radio. During January of 1995 she visited our city and delivered a lecture on "Understanding Washington." I attended, motivated by her reputation and my consistent confusion about what exactly is going on in our nation's capital.

The timing of her lecture coincided with debate in Congress on the Balanced Budget Amendment. She observed that for years lawmakers have known that tough decisions must be made to balance the budget. Rather than make those commitments, they chose instead to expend their energy passing an amendment that would force them to make the necessary commitments. In a display of what she labeled "magical thinking," a commitment to (at some point in the future) make commitments is the focal point of national legislation.

Making commitments is not just a national difficulty, it is a personal one as well. You and I sense that making and keeping commitments is valuable, yet we are bombarded with the impression that commitments are restrictive. Like shopping for interest rates on a mortgage, you fear a better deal will come along and you will miss it if you "lock in."

Can you forge lasting commitments in a world where values and lifestyles are constantly shifting? Absolutely! But you must continually challenge existing perceptions of commitment that undermine your resolve. Then, armed with a knowledge of the building blocks of commitment provided by the writer of Ecclesiastes, you will be equipped to carefully formulate character-building and life-enriching commitments.

PERCEPTION HAS A WAY OF BECOMING REALITY

Have you noticed the different ways people perceive commitments? Many view them as burdens—especially the long-term ones, like marriage.

Our local newspaper recently carried an article entitled, "Marriage Option Outdated, Invalid For Many Who Live Together." One person quoted in the article was especially forthright: "I never want to get married. I never want to have children. None of those encumbrances." What caught my attention was not his choices regarding marriage and parenting, but how openly these historically valued commitments were pronounced as "excess baggage"— encumbrances to be avoided if at all possible.

Another perception is that of being overwhelmed by all the possible options. I have experienced this frustration with regard to long-distance telephone service. It seems as if once a week my dinner is interrupted by a long-distance carrier who has "a deal" for me. I have gotten to the point I don't even care anymore, even if it will save me a few dollars.

While that may not be a serious concern when it comes to long-distance service, it bothers me more to realize that I am also beginning to feel this way about giving. I do not know if charitable organizations swap mailing lists, but my mail so regularly includes pleas for money that sometimes I no longer even bother opening them. It is not that these are not worthy causes or quality organizations. Rather, I am tired, or have grown numb, because of the proliferation of options for my personal giving. This "option explosion" leads many of us to say "No" more quickly and others to say "Yes" with no intention of following through. Either of these responses can be habit-forming, and less than satisfying.

Another perception is that commitments correspond to certain phases of life. The practice of "serial monogamy" is one evidence. A man chooses a spouse to enjoy his youth with, but may not see her as a suitable mother. So he divorces her and marries someone to bear his children. She, however, may not be the one he wants to enjoy the empty nest with, so he divorces and marries again. He is monogamous when married, but marries and divorces depending on his phase in life. While not decided consciously, it is reality in their lives.

I see this most often in the matter of church membership. Most people no longer view church membership as a lifelong commitment, but as something appropriate for a particular life situation. When a family has young children, they choose a church with a good children's program. When their kids are teenagers, they opt for the church with the "happening" youth groups. When the kids are gone, it's time to join the church with active senior adult ministries. Lifelong membership in a spiritually dead church can be detrimental to your relationship with God, but changing churches with every change in life undermines a sense of belonging and faithfulness.

If you put these perceptions together, it becomes evident why we hesitate to make lasting commitments: We anticipate feeling restricted and overwhelmed. This, however, is where perception fails to match reality.

There is a paradox in promise-making and promise-keeping. What appears to be confining is really freeing. Lasting commitments lead to lasting meaning in life. Enduring satisfaction in every dimension of life comes when you make the right commitments and keep those commitments. Giving and keeping your word may mean delaying gratification, but that is the pathway to lasting gratification. Life is deeper and better with commitments fulfilled than with sporadic experiences of immediate gratification.

What appears restrictive can actually be the means to freedom. I bump into this obstacle consistently when I ask couples during premarital counseling whether or not they have a written financial budget. Because it takes a bit of work and forces couples to agree on how to invest limited resources, more often than not the answer is "No." A budget *seems* restrictive.

Suppose they decide to give budgeting a try. They talk about how much they should spend in one area of the budget—let's say clothes. Suppose, in this case, the man says $2000 a year (he likes nice suits) and the woman says $500 a year (she likes low-cost casual). Rather than coming to agreement and commitment in their budget (which feels restrictive), they decide to postpone finishing the budget (they don't have a balanced budget amendment).

What happens? He spends $2000 a year on clothes. She does not want to spend that much on clothes, but if he is going to spend $2000 on clothes, she decides to spend that much on furniture. This spending exceeds their income, but credit cards help them postpone facing reality. I see them a year or so after their wedding because they are constantly fighting about money. Their credit cards carry maximum balances and they are making minimum payments. Larger dreams of a home or new car seem even more remote than before they were married. Agreement and commitment early on would have meant freedom from pressure in their relationship and freedom to pursue their biggest dreams. Instant gratification undermines lasting satisfaction.

Ultimately your character is a reflection of your commitments. It is built up when you make and keep commitments and weakened when you simply respond to the whims of the moment. In making and keeping commitments, you will encounter resistance. That resistance can strengthen your character, just as resistance in exercising develops muscle fiber. Overcoming natural resistance and developing intentional perseverance is vital to "top of the line" living.

FORGING LASTING COMMITMENTS

In Ecclesiastes 5:1–7 we discover that the Teacher's search finally takes him to church. His investigation moves from the horizontal to the vertical. He pictures a well-meaning man who goes to church but listens with half an ear and never quite gets around to doing what he said he would do. Perhaps you fit that picture. You faithfully attend church, hoping to find more meaning there than you have found in other places you have looked. You are looking for commitments that will bring meaning to your life weekdays as well as Sundays, yet you are not sure how that might come about. That is the setting in which the writer of Ecclesiastes develops four steps in forging lasting commitments:

Step 1: Proceed with Caution

The author's first building block of commitment may surprise you. It is not a motivational pep talk, but a word of warning:

> *Guard your steps when you go to the house of God. Go near to listen rather than to offer the sacrifice of fools, who do not know that they do wrong.*
>
> *Do not be quick with your mouth,*
> *do not be hasty in your heart*
> *to utter anything before God.* (5:1–2)

Proceed with caution, he says. "Guard your steps. ... Go near to listen. ... Do not be quick with your mouth, do not be hasty in your heart." The longer and greater the commitment, the more caution is required. It takes time for significant commitments to germinate. Like seed in the garden, the action begins beneath the surface before anyone is able to see the results.

New commitments may take weeks, months, or even years to formulate in your mind and heart. Almost subconsciously you increase your motivation by building a list of reasons to make a commitment–the "pros." Simultaneously you reduce the internal barriers to change–the "cons." You are talking yourself into taking action by amassing will power and building internal resolve.

During this time, whatever is marinating in your mind is evolving from a "good idea someday" to a matter of conviction. Short-circuiting this step is fraught with danger. It is a trap. "It is a trap for a man to dedicate something rashly and only later to consider his vows" (Proverbs 20:25). Those are words of wisdom for bottom-line, action-oriented men.

The first step, then, is to "go near to listen." Listening in God's presence is more than simply hearing. The writer of Ecclesiastes has carefully chosen a word that carries double force: "listening with the intention of obeying." A sense of conviction does not come from talking loud and long, but from truly hearing what your heart has to say and then conditioning your will to commit to it.

One day when Jesus was teaching, his disciples noticed the large crowd drawing near. They thought this would be a great opportunity to get some of these seekers to sign on the dotted line. How did Christ respond? He used two stories to challenge them to "count the cost" (see Luke 14:28–33). If a man is going to build a tower, he had better count the cost first. It would be embarrassing to have to quit halfway because he did not carefully assess his resources. Or again, if a king is going to war, he had better count his troops and estimate his enemy's strength. If he is unable to win, he had better negotiate. Then Christ shares the bottom line: If anyone is serious about following me, he or she had better count the cost. Being part of the crowd is easy, but being a fully devoted follower is another matter. There is a world of difference between an afternoon's entertainment (good teaching and a few miracles) and a lifetime of commitment. Count the cost. Proceed with caution.

The purpose of caution is to build conviction. Do not confuse caution with procrastination. This is not an excuse for delaying what needs to be done, nor is it a time to rationalize indecision. We are all prone to fear when faced with change. This step is not for justifying our fears, but for fortifying our faith.

Step 2: Signal Your Intentions

This second step is the time to go public with your plans.

Do not be quick with your mouth,
do not be hasty in your heart
to utter anything before God.
God is in heaven
and you are on earth,
so let your words be few.
As a dream comes when there are many cares,
so the speech of a fool when there are many words.

(5:2–3)

At first glance you might conclude the author is telling you to keep your thoughts to yourself. Yet he assumes commitments will be communicated and suggests we verbalize them not by waxing eloquent but by using simple and clear expression.

It is true that we live in a world that is better at "mouthing" commitments than "making" them. It is also true, to quote Linda Wertheimer again, that "nothing is as tough as living with answered prayer." We need to be careful about what we ask for, because God just might give it to us! But the time for caution is the first step; the time to go public is the second.

Dr. James Prochaska, a University of Rhode Island psychology professor, underscores the importance of speaking up:

> There comes a point (about a month before attempting a drastic behavioral change) when it's important to publicly state intentions. Many people don't go public because they're afraid they'll fail–this actually weakens their will-power. Public commitments are much stronger.[1]

Prochaska is echoing what the Bible says to those seeking to make a commitment to Christ: "For it is with your heart that you believe and are justified, and it is with your mouth that you confess and are saved" (Romans 10:10).

While churches tend to emphasize the commitment of the heart (step 1), equal weight is given in this verse to what is confessed to others (step 2). Whether it be a life-changing commitment to Christ, a decision to quit smoking, or a goal to be home on time for supper, it is strengthened when it is openly communicated.

This is one of the reasons I have never bought into the idea that religion is a private matter, that "my relationship with God is just between him and me." We have all been offended by hypocrites, who say one thing but do another, or by people who preach their commitments at others. Yet what if you, with humility and simplicity, said to your coworkers, "I value honesty and kindness, and I seek to honor God with my life. If you ever see something that causes you to question whether I am living out these values, please bring it to my attention. I want my walk to match my talk." You would certainly have their attention—and accountability!

In Alcoholics Anonymous a common adage is "you are as sick as you are secretive." Communicating commitments can be a bit embarrassing as you reveal areas that need to change and struggles that you have encountered in previous attempts. Many churches subtly pressure people to keep their secrets, and many families do the same. Open communication is a sign of health and provides strength for new endeavors in personal growth.

Keep your announcement of intentions simple. "Let your 'Yes' be 'Yes'" (Matthew 5:37; James 5:12), and resist the extremes of understatement or overstatement. Choose your audience carefully. As Zig Ziglar has often noted in his speeches,

> If it's a "give up" goal, tell everyone. Both your cheerleaders and your critics will be glad to remind you if you vary from your diet plan. But if it's a "go up" goal, representing new territory in personal growth, tell only a few who believe in you and will encourage you. Keep your critics in the dark because they'll discourage (drain the courage from) you.

Step 3: Keep Your Commitment Consistently

You have thought about it and you have talked about it; now it is time to do it.

> *When you make a vow to God, do not delay in fulfilling it. He has no pleasure in fools; fulfill your vow. It is better not to vow than to make a vow and not fulfill it. Do not let your mouth lead you into sin. And do not protest to the temple messenger, "My vow was a mistake." (5:4–6a)*

The time for living and fulfilling commitments has come. The writer of Ecclesiastes says, "Do not delay in fulfilling [your word]" (5:4); "Do not protest [when you've given your word]" (5:6). You have made a promise; now keep it consistently.

Do not confuse keeping commitments consistently and keeping them perfectly; these two concepts are worlds apart. Perfectionism prevents you from ever making commitments because we are imperfect people in an imperfect world. In fact, failure often comes sooner than expected. The most likely time to relapse into former patterns is immediately after you have announced your commitment and are still adjusting to the changes it brings. Consistency says, "I will try my best, though I will fail." When you do, acknowledge your inconsistency, seek forgiveness if necessary, and return to commitment-keeping. God and others do not expect perfection, but their understanding and forgiveness should motivate us to live so that every day that passes your commitments become more and more a habit–not only part of what you do, but also part of who you are.

The issue is not learning more, it is living more. No gimmick can substitute for discipline. I watched with fascination a recent TV special on infomercials. The whole goal of those who sponsor these programs is to convince us that if we had their product (to slice our vegetables, dye our hair, build positive thoughts), our lives would be richer or simpler. While they may contain a measure of truth, they often appeal to our search for shortcuts. I sometimes wonder if modern society's mad dash for self-help materials and the proliferation of motivation seminars is not evidence of a desire to be distracted from the basics. We seek a no-risk, no-discipline success.

I see this frequently with people who want to go into business to "be successful like someone else." They fantasize about and glamorize business ownership. They are in for a surprise! I see behind the scenes into the lives of many business owners. The early years of a business start-up involve unsettling risks, tough-minded persever-ance, and incredible energy. Even the later years can involve uncertainty and worry. If a person believes the pathway is a risk-free, easy-does-it endeavor that leads only to the freedom of setting your own hours and making lots of money, it will be a rude awakening.

Bill Gates is one of the best known businessmen in America. His company, Microsoft, is an aggressive competitor and stellar performer in the business world. *Forbes* writers followed him around for a few days and concluded:

> Einstein once said the most noble human trait was "the ability to rise above mere existence by sacrificing one's self through the years for a goal." Gates possesses this trait. To a degree rare among other large company CEOs, he is remarkably indifferent to whether he is eating hamburger or steak, flying coach or first class, taking cab or limo, staying in an ordinary room or presidential suite, sitting on a cheap plastic seat or richly stuffed leather, being fawned over or not. What turns on Bill Gates is learning, competing, and Microsoft.[2]

Whether Gates's priorities are right is arguable, but his consistency in pursuing them is legendary.

It is not talking that translates your commitments into character. Your values are not simply a matter of what you say. If I say I love my wife but never make time for her, do I truly value her? No. If I say I have a good work ethic but squander time and shirk responsibility, do I value a good work ethic? Hardly! In reality, many people who talk most stridently about certain commitments fail to live them consistently.

It is not talking but acting with increasing consistency that develops "muscle memory." Like a golfer who swings a club again and again, repetition builds the necessary muscle memory. (Unfortunately, when it comes to golf, my muscles suffer from memory loss!) Does this ensure perfection? Not for any golfers I have encountered! It does increase the predictability of his game, so that more and more he trusts his swing. Trust is not built with words with but with actions. Practice does not make one perfect, but it does make one more consistent. Just do it—again and again.

Step 4: The Vertical Edge

The writer of Ecclesiastes leads us to the bottom line of commitment: "Much dreaming and many words are meaningless. Therefore stand in awe of God" (5:7). There is something about focusing on a commitment-keeping God that empowers us to forge worthwhile commitments.

What "awes" you helps indicate what is at the center of your life. Some men stand in awe of themselves. Their life commitments are an ego trip, and, as Ken Blanchard puts it, EGO results in "Edging God Out." These people make and keep self-serving commitments. As a man involved in Alcoholics Anonymous observed, "A.A. works for people who believe in God. A.A. even works for people who don't believe in God. But A.A. doesn't work for the man who believes he is God."

Some men stand in awe of nothing. The center of their lives is empty. Their commitments are based on external circumstances. In a world churning with change, they often come to the conclusion that long-term commitments are impossible. They lack what Stephen Covey calls the "changeless core," rendering them incapable of the inner strength and stability essential to commitment.

Whirlwind change can intimidate even those with allegiance to a changeless God. Recently I taught a graduate class on "change management" for pastors. I could not help but notice the uncertainty in many of their faces. Their parishioners no longer seemed to respect who they were or what they had to say. Their roles as leaders in a spiritual community seemed outdated in a world of unrestrained individualism. They were scrambling to meet the demands of church members whose consumer mentality dictated stimulating sermons, innovative programs, and high-tech, high-touch ministry.

Early in the class I shared what has become the foundation of long-term ministry for me. If you "stand in awe of God," most of what is important in life and ministry never changes. That is true wherever you work. Your work station may change, technology will change, and organizational structures will evolve and require new skills. But the most important qualities—a life of integrity, a strong work ethic, treating people with dignity—arise out of the changeless core that is constantly reenergized in the presence of God. If there is nothing at the center, there is no anchoring point. Everything is adrift.

Standing in awe of God frees you from the reign of false gods, from frantically seeking to meet all the expectations of others, from self-reliance, from climbing the corporate ladder—just to name a few. Forging every commitment in life in the presence of God gives us the vertical edge, an orienting principle in life.

Every commitment in life should reflect your commitment to God. Your commitment to your wife should not be based on how she responds to you. Your standard for commitment should be to "love [her] just as Christ loved the church" (Ephesians 5:25). Your commitment to your employer should not be based on how he treats you. "Whatever you do, work at it with all your heart, as working for the Lord, not for men, since you know that you will receive an inheritance from the Lord as a reward. It is the Lord Christ you are serving." (Colossians 3:23–24). Standing in awe of God becomes a daily prayer and exercise as you seek to do his will in honoring your commitments to him, to your family and friends, and to those purposes to which he has called you.

This final step of consecration does more than create consistency between your walk and your talk. It creates a match between what is going on within you and what is going on around you. It leads to the integration of your public world and private world. Keeping commitments becomes God's work within you. No amount of willpower will ever substitute for the power of a life transformed by the presence of God.

TEN COMMANDMENTS FOR COMMITMENTS

1 *"You shall have no other gods before me."* Borrowed from the original Ten Commandments, this commitment is the foundation of all others. Effective promise-keepers have a covenant-keeping God at the center of their lives.

2 *"In times of crisis, do not underestimate the value of even the simplest commitments."* On a bad day, avoiding doing something stupid can be a major victory!

3 *"Nurture a commitment-keeping mentality by faithfulness in little things."* If you say you will call someone, call them. If you say you will drop them a note by the end of the week, write it. If you say, "Let's do lunch sometime," do it. "Whoever can be trusted with very little can also be trusted with much, and whoever is dishonest with very little will also be dishonest with much" (Luke 16:10).

4 *"Exercise caution when joining others in a commitment."* Mark Kimball, CEO of Gus Macker Enterprises, once shared with me that "you cannot make a good deal with a bad person." No matter how good it seems, if the person's character is questionable, the commitment will be questionable. Do not believe the myth that says, "I'll change them" (e.g., "I'll change her after we're married"; "I'll change him after we're partners in business"). Apart from the occasional miracle, this is a fantasy with painful consequences.

5 *"Know the terms of your commitment."* The longer the term, the greater the thought and prayer that should be given. There should be a noticeable difference between choosing your breakfast cereal and choosing your new house. The results of one will be digested by noon, the other you will pay on for years to come.

6 *"Teach your children to make and keep commitments."* If we allow them to drop off a sports team at the first sign of difficulty or avoid a school subject that will appropriately challenge them, we are only setting them up for future difficulties with commitments. Teach them the four steps of commitment-making that the writer of Ecclesiastes has outlined for us.

7 *"Seek forgiveness for lapsed commitments."* If you have made a commitment and failed to honor it, ask for forgiveness. Offer to make restitution if the situation calls for it. If the forgiveness you need is from God, he will provide it and enable you to make a new beginning. "If we confess our sins, he is faithful and just and will forgive us our sins and purify us from all unrighteousness" (1 John 1:9). Reaffirm lapsed commitments.

8. *"Seek to establish accountability for your commitments."* My accountability to a trusted partner over the last decade has been essential to my faithfulness in honoring my commitments. Meeting regularly with another individual or small group will provide a setting to "go public with your intentions" and to be monitored in your actions. We do what is inspected, not what is expected.

9 *"Celebrate commitments when they are kept."* Do not focus only on the areas in which you have struggled, and do not simply fulfill a commitment and move quickly to the next. Take time to celebrate the anniversaries and mark the milestones of lasting commitments.

10 *"Do not make commitments a do-it-yourself project."* Stand in awe of God. Make sure your commitments reflect his will in the first place. Then trust him to provide the strength you need and ask him for his resources of faithfulness, hope, and patience. Our inability to follow through should not prevent us from establishing significant commitments, but should motivate us humbly to pursue them in reliance on God.

NOTES

1. James Prochaska, *Changing For God*, as reported by Tim Whitmire, "In 1995 I Vow to ... ," *The Grand Rapids Press* (December 27, 1994), p. A3.

2. Rich Karlgaard, "On the Road with Bill Gates," *Forbes ASAP* (February 28, 1994), p. 80.

7

Money ... The More the Merrier?

SCRIPTURE: ECCLESIASTES 5:10–20

I have provided leadership in hundreds of church services and have discovered that some things happen in church that cause people to cringe.

- A soloist who does not quite find her note but holds it loud and long anyway
- A wrong accompaniment tape, so that everything stops while the correct tape is found
- A member of the drama team who forgets his line, and nervous silence prevails until the prompter gets him on track again
- An illustration in my message that embarrasses people rather than emphasizes my point

These are "cringe factors."

Just addressing certain topics can cause people to cringe. Mother's Day sentiments can tear at the heart of an infertile married woman. The subject of sin makes people squirm, especially if it speaks to those sins Christians commonly struggle with, yet cover up. Put "sin" together with "hell," and you will raise the anxiety level of the audience. However, the "king of cringe" is money. Defenses go up right along with everybody's blood pressure.

God is not against money. He just wants you to think clearly about what it can and cannot do. He wants you never to forget its ability to attach itself to the very core of who you are. In the words of Jesus, "For where your treasure is, there your heart will be also" (Matthew 6:21).

Money makes a lousy lover, but it has an uncanny ability to capture your heart. Learn to respect the awesome power of money. While it is nothing but pieces of paper, it influences everything in life—your character, your priorities, your relationships. It never ceases to amaze me what a man will trade for money. It is the way we keep score in a man's world; it is the bottom line.

The writer of Ecclesiastes places the issue clearly in front of you. Either you will pursue the fantasies money generates, or you will face the hard realities of money and capitalize on them. The choice you make about money's place in your life will determine what you trade for it, and the consequences of your choice can be positive or negative. One thing is certain: Those consequences will be more than financial. They will be emotional, relational, even spiritual.

This chapter is not about managing money; it is about the mirages of money. God's view of money and the conclusions men come to about money apart from God are often worlds apart. The world lies to us, but God tells us the truth.

Even men most committed to God's way struggle intermittently with the mirages of money. You will not move into reality, the "above the sun" perspective, once and for all. You and I will drift into the "financial fantasy" world; thus, we will need to do periodic reality checks.

FINANCIAL FANTASIES AND REALITY CHECKS

Financial Fantasy #1: A little more and I'd be satisfied (5:10)

Surveys show that no matter how much money a man makes, he tends to tell himself that if he had just a little more, he would be satisfied. That is true whether his annual income is $25,000 or $125,000. Once he gets that next raise he will be content–until he gets it, and then he starts anticipating the next one.

What is the relationship between money and contentment? The Bible talks a lot about money and much about contentment. Sometimes it even discusses the two together. Its conclusion?

Does money = contentment? No.
Does poverty = contentment? No.

In fact, there is no direct relationship between money and contentment. You know wealthy people who are happy and wealthy people who are miserable. You know people with limited financial resources who are happy and such people who are miserable.

There is no direct relationship between money and contentment except that *the more you expect from money, the less it delivers.* In the words of Ecclesiastes:

Whoever loves money never has money enough;
*   whoever loves wealth is never satisfied with his income.*
*   This too is meaningless.* (5:10)

Money makes a lousy lover. The more you love it, the less it satisfies. The more you focus on it, the less it delivers.

One of the most insightful interviews I have ever witnessed was conducted by Barbara Walters with David Geffen. While I do not agree with Geffen on everything, his insights into money are profound. David was a millionaire at age twenty-five, a personal manager for such stars as Bob Dylan, The Doors, James Taylor, and Linda Ronstadt. He retired in the 1970s when he was only in his mid-thirties. He came out of retirement to found Geffen Records in 1980, which went on to become the most successful independent record company in history, signing stars like Elton John and John Lennon. He sold his company and is now worth over one billion dollars. Most recently he has created a movie studio with Steven Spielberg and Jeffrey Katzenberg, two of the biggest names in the business. Here is an excerpt from that *20/20* interview:

Barbara Walters: What did the money mean to you?

David Geffen: It meant freedom. It meant I would never have to worry about money again.

Walters: Did it mean you were happy?

Geffen: No. Happy is harder than money. Anybody who thinks money will make you happy doesn't have money.

Geffen has been there and has it. Yet he is realistic about what money can do and cannot do. It can provide a measure of freedom, but it cannot provide happiness. Money by itself does not satisfy. The key is what you can combine it with; some combinations work, others do not. "Happy is harder than money."

Do not give money a place it cannot fill. Do not create expectations it cannot meet. Above all, do not love it. Loving money unleashes nothing but trouble. "For the love of money is a root of all kinds of evil" (I Timothy 6:10).

Reality Check #1: Contentment is a gift of God (5:19–20)

If the number one priority of your life is to be wealthy, you will never be content. If the number one priority of your life is to pursue God's design for you, he gives you a wonderful gift:

> *Moreover, when God gives any man wealth and possessions, and enables him to enjoy them, to accept his lot and to be happy in his work–this is a gift of God. He seldom reflects on the days of his life, because God keeps him occupied with gladness of heart.* (5:19–20)

God is prepared to give two gifts to the man who acknowledges him. He not only gives you things, he also gives you the ability to enjoy those things.

We once had a guy break into our church to steal whatever he could sell to finance his cocaine habit. He stole from us to finance a moment of happiness that would not last. The futility of his actions was obvious to all. But how much difference is there between the guy who robbed our church to buy "happiness" and the guy who robs his family by working eighty hours a week to buy happiness? It may be more socially acceptable, but it is equally futile. Happiness is a gift that cannot be stolen or earned.

The ebullient Ray Charles was once baited by a *60 Minutes* interviewer with a question about the inequity between his earnings and those of white entertainers. The question had overtones of racism and would have tugged at the heart of any man who was greedy. Ray's answer was disarming: "I make a good living. I can only ride in one car at a time, live in one house at a time, sleep with one woman at a time" (I trust it was his wife). Ray is right, and he is also content.

Better one handful with tranquillity
than two handfuls with toil
and chasing after the wind. ...
There was a man all alone;
he had neither son nor brother.
There was no end to his toil,
yet his eyes were not content with his wealth.
"For whom am I toiling," he asked,
"and why am I depriving myself of enjoyment?"
This too is meaningless—
a miserable business! (4:6, 8)

There is nothing wrong with having money, but loving money is the roadway to meaninglessness. Contentment is a gift of God that cannot be earned but certainly can be enjoyed.

Financial Fantasy #2: Money can make my worries go away (5:11–12)

This fantasy is especially tempting to those who have overextended themselves through the use of debt—a growing percentage of the population! If you have any financial track record at all, offers for credit cards with increasingly high limits are part of your weekly mail. Advertisers are sophisticated and subtle in stimulating our desires to spend. While it is common to blame easy credit or effective advertising, that is really a distraction from the central issue.

As goods increase,
so do those who consume them.
And what benefit are they to the owner
except to feast his eyes on them?

The sleep of a laborer is sweet,
  whether he eats little or much,
but the abundance of a rich man
  permits him no sleep. (5:11–12)

What is the issue? Consumption. As your resources increase, so does your desire and opportunity to consume them. As you consume more and more, you begin to be consumed. And being consumed with what you have or what you owe interrupts your sleep with worry. The attitude that "money will make my worries go away" misleads us to believe our worries are related to the income side of the ledger. The writer of Ecclesiastes prompts us to examine the expense side of the ledger.

105 percent = frustration

If you spend 105% of your income, making up the difference with borrowing, financial worries increase.

95 percent = relaxation

If you spend 95 percent of your income, putting the difference into savings, financial "breathing room" increases. The difference between worry and freedom rests in changing your consumption patterns by only a few percentage points.

Simple as it seems, most people do not see it. According to family researcher Delores Curran, 58 percent of married men and 66 percent of married women list finances as one of the top stresses in their family. Most believe the issue is a lack of money. But in the words of Epicurus, the ancient Greek philosopher, "Add not to a man's possessions, but take away from his desires."

In 1994 *Forbes* magazine published an article entitled "The Tyranny of Possessions." It highlighted rich individuals who had purchased their dream vacation homes, yachts, or aircraft, only to conclude it was not worth the hassle.

To escape the problem of these expensive possessions consuming their time, money, and energy, they concluded that "most of the very best things in life can be rented." They discovered the burden of possessions can outweigh the pleasures. What you own can consume you. Wealth can create worries instead of solving them.

Reality Check #2: Trusting God makes my worries go away

The answer to worry is found in your pocket! It is not the amount of money that is there, but what is printed on the money: "IN GOD WE TRUST." That motto is consistent with the words of Jesus:

> *Therefore I tell you, do not worry about your life, what you will eat or drink; or about your body, what you will wear. Is not life more important than food, and the body more important than clothes? . . . For the pagans run after all these things, and your heavenly Father knows that you need them. But seek first his kingdom and his righteousness, and all these things will be given to you as well. Therefore do not worry about tomorrow, for tomorrow will worry about itself. Each day has enough trouble of its own.* (Matthew 6:25, 32–34)

One of the distinguishing characteristics between a man who trusts God and one who does not is found in what he pursues to remedy his worry. If you do not trust God, you will spend your energy "running after things." If you do trust God, you will spend your energy on things important to him and will trust him to show you what you really need; he will then supply it. Where you place your trust and how you face your worries will determine your life's activities. The writer of Ecclesiastes knew this:

> *To the man who pleases him, God gives wisdom, knowledge and happiness, but to the sinner he gives the tasks of gathering and storing up wealth to hand it over to the one who pleases God. This too is meaningless, a chasing after the wind.* (2:26)

Our worries increase as the "mirage of more" consumes us. Our worries dissipate as God becomes the focus of our lives and the supplier of our needs.

A good friend of mine in the financial planning field believes men make a tragic mistake when their consumption is determined by what they make or what they can borrow. He instead encourages men to determine a "lifestyle lid" that reflects God's will for their spending. He cautions that excessive frugality is not a sign of spirituality, nor is excessive spending healthy even if the resources are available. Seek God's will for what you save, what you give, and what you spend. That is what creates true security and eliminates needless worry.

Financial Fantasy #3: Everyone values and uses money in the same way (5:13–14)

Making the most of money is complex because no two people view it the same way. Susan Forward, a therapist and best-selling author, calls money "an emotional diverter valve," a buffer protecting us from our hidden insecurities. If you are fighting about money or doing self-destructive things with money, 99 percent of the time it is not about money; rather, it is about you or your partner. She views money as a metaphor for who you really are as a person.

It is those emotional issues that are manifested in how we use money. The writer of Ecclesiastes is aware of how different the natural tendencies of people can be when it comes to money:

"I have seen a grievous evil under the sun:

wealth hoarded to the harm of its owner,
or wealth lost through some misfortune." (5:13–14a)

He identifies two ends of the continuum. On one end are those who hoard, who are focused on accumulating assets. Their security is in their savings. While appropriate savings is helpful, hoarding is harmful. There is a simple test to determine the difference between saving and hoarding: "Saving without giving is hoarding." If you are so focused on saving that you cannot be generous in meeting legitimate needs or furthering legitimate causes, you are hoarding. As John Wesley taught, "Make all you can. Save all you can. Give all you can." He went on to observe that all of his followers were excited about "making all you can." Most of his followers were enthusiastic about "saving all you can." But enthusiasm dropped off noticeably when it came to "giving all you can"! Frugality without generosity constitutes harmful hoarding.

On the other end of the continuum from hoarding is speculating. If the hoarder avoids all risks, the speculator assumes unreasonable risks that may well result in misfortune.

One of the most dramatic examples of the consequences of speculation is the Casa Loma in the city of Toronto. My wife and I toured this beautiful castle constructed by Sir Henry Mill Pellatt, a prominent Toronto financier, industrialist, and military man. An unabashed romantic, Sir Henry created this castle overlooking the city. Begun in 1911, it took three hundred men nearly three years to complete and cost $3.5 million at that time. But Sir Henry enjoyed Casa Loma less than ten years before financial misfortune due to speculative investments forced him to abandon his castle home and liquidate everything he owned – right down to his invalid wife's wheelchair. While on a grander scale than most, Sir Henry is but one of many men whose desire to get rich quick or to live beyond their means resulted in misfortune.

I have discovered something about natural tendencies:

- We assume others view and use money like us, projecting our tendencies onto them. In reality, most couples I marry prove that "opposites attract." The person who cannot hang on to a dollar forms a life partnership with a person who cannot let go of a dollar.
- Those with church backgrounds tend to spiritualize their natural tendencies. Hoarding becomes "good stewardship"; speculating becomes "an act of faith." God becomes an excuse for our excesses.
- The best long-term strategy for personal well-being is somewhere between the extremes of hoarding and speculating. Once you know your natural tendency, you need to moderate it by creating a more balanced approach to money.

We grow as we become aware of our natural tendencies. Learn to discipline them and to recognize the natural tendencies of others.

Reality Check #3: How you value and use money speaks volumes about you

Money has a way of revealing what is in your heart: "For where your treasure is, there your heart will be also"

(Matthew 6:21). Since money says a lot about you, you should listen to what it is saying:

- If money is your source of security, your emotional well-being is resting on a shaky foundation.
- If money is your source of identity, your self-worth will never exceed your net worth.
- If money is the ultimate recipient of your loyalty, it will eventually master you.

One of the greatest investments of time you can make is writing a brief "money autobiography." Think about who managed the money in your family of origin and what messages they communicated about money. Look at your patterns of money usage and ask what it communicates about you. Then use these insights to make the necessary changes so that money says what you want about your values and priorities.

Financial Fantasy #4: Money has enduring value (5:15–17)

On the surface we all recognize the fallacy of this fantasy. Yet subconsciously we tend to treat money as if it will be around forever, and as if we will be too. This is evidenced in what we are willing to trade for it.

In their book *The Day America Told the Truth*, researchers James Patterson and Peter Kim asked people, "What are you honestly willing to do for $10 million." Twenty-five percent said they would abandon their entire family. Twenty-three percent would become prostitutes for a week or more, and seven percent would kill a stranger. A follow-up survey revealed that at $5 million, $4 million, and $3 million the answers were similar. It was not until they got below $2 million that they saw a significant decline in what people would do for money. The authors concluded, "Our price in America seems to be $2 million or thereabouts." That is the price at which people trade things of lasting value (like family relationships or personal morality) for a sum of money.

If you trade something of lasting significance for money, it indicates you believe money will make a more lasting difference in your life. Money itself is not the issue; it is what you are willing to trade for it. In the words of the common adage, "Money isn't everything, but it sure beats whatever's second!"

Reality Check #4: You can't take it with you

The writer of Ecclesiastes challenges us never to forget that money is temporary, but life is eternal.

Naked a man comes from his mother's womb,
  and as he comes, so he departs.
He takes nothing from his labor
  that he can carry in his hand.
This too is a grievous evil:
As a man comes, so he departs,
  and what does he gain,
  since he toils for the wind? (5:15–16)

The accountant of John D. Rockefeller, the financial magnate, put it even more succinctly. When asked how much Rockefeller left behind, his one-word answer said it all: "Everything." The answer will be the same for you and me.

Several years ago my wife and I toured Egypt. We briefly visited the National Museum of Egypt ("briefly" is my favorite way to visit museums) in Cairo. Our guide described to us the ancient customs of burial, including people being buried with their valuables. As a result, their tombs were filled with jewelry, food items, furniture – even some servants were buried with their masters! This represented the futile attempts of ancient Egyptians to take their possessions with them into the next world.

The best way to "take it with you" is not to tuck it away in your casket, but to invest it in ways that bring eternal returns. We should channel our resources into that which lasts–the lives of people and the purposes of God.

Financial Fantasy #5: I can control my financial future, or I'm a self-made man (5:18–19)

One of the most powerful drives in the lives of men is the need to control. When you link the need to control with the tendency of men to "keep score" with money and possessions, we begin to believe we are masters of our financial fate; we are captains of our ships.

In reality, Ecclesiastes says we are "toiling for the wind." What a powerful comparison: Our efforts to prosper are similar to chasing the wind! Money, like the wind, is really nothing, but it impacts everything. Money is simply a piece of paper, yet it makes and breaks men. It makes and breaks marriages. It makes and breaks companies and ministries. Its effects are witnessed in every dimension of life, yet it is as elusive as the wind.

Navigating your financial future is like a pilot guiding an aircraft. If he channels the wind properly, it ensures a successful flight. But a good pilot never loses respect for the wind; he knows a headwind will slow him down and a tail-wind will speed him up. He realizes wind shear can slam his plane to the ground. So he constantly monitors the wind, making the most of it while never believing he has conquered it.

So too you must never lose respect for the changing winds of financial well-being. A period of financial success can lull you into believing you are in control. Many a man has failed in business because, having succeeded with one business, he automatically assumed success would be repeated in another. He forgot that financial prosperity involves not only things he can control, but also forces he cannot control. A glance at the following chart reminds us of our limitations:

Can Control	*Can't Control*
• Continued development of skills through reading, mentoring from others, and educational opportunities	• Our health and life span
• Continued improvement of products and service through sensitivity to customer needs and awareness of new approaches	• Overall economic conditions, such as inflation or recession
• The proper management of resources.	• Changing demand based on technological advances.

A wise man humbly determines his part and yet recognizes the part only God can control.

Reality Check #5: Financial blessing is a gift and a trust

You need to realize what the writer of Ecclesiastes realized:

> *Then I realized that it is good and proper for a man to eat and drink, and to find satisfaction in his toilsome labor under the sun during the few days of life God has given him—for this is his lot. Moreover, when God gives any man wealth and*

possessions, and enables him to enjoy them, to
accept his lot and be happy in his work–this is a
gift of God. (5:18–19)

The days of your life are a gift. Wealth and possessions are a gift. Accepting and enjoying your resources are a gift. A gift cannot be earned and controlled. It can be gratefully accepted and then invested in ways that honor the giver. The healthiest way to make the most of money is to see it as a gift to be enjoyed and a trust to be managed.

Jerry Tubergen is the accountant selected by Richard DeVos to help manage some of the DeVos family's substantial resources. Jerry's role provides a wonderful living for his family as well as numerous opportunities for travel and enjoyment as part of his responsibilities. Jerry enjoys the best seats in the house at Orlando Magic games (the DeVos family owns the Magic).

While enjoying the "perks" of his position, Jerry does not lose sight of his purpose–to invest the resources he has been entrusted with and to manage them in a way that benefits the owner. His job is to know what the owner expects. There are some investments others might make that he will not because he knows they are inconsistent with the owner's standards and values. He is a steward of what belongs to someone else.

In a similar way, we have been given the responsibility of managing a portion of what belongs to a fabulously wealthy Owner–God himself. That responsibility includes the gift of a living for our family and wonderful opportunities to make the most of each day. We must also know what the Owner expects, and then invest this trust in a way consistent with his standards and values. God gives us a gift–a "trust" fund. You are the manager.

GETTING YOUR MONEY'S WORTH

It is time to conduct an "audit" of your attitudes, your actions, and your achievements. Here are some areas to address in your audit report:

1. Hook up the heart monitor. What is going on inside? Are you content, or are you consumed by financial concerns?
2. Test your tendencies. Are you a "hoarder" by nature or more of a "speculator"?
3. Check your pressure valve. Is the use of debt extending you beyond your means, or are you experiencing the freedom of living within your means?

Dr. James Dobson, founder of Focus on the Family, shares:

> I have concluded that the accumulation of wealth, even if I could achieve it, is an insufficient reason for living. When I reach the end of my days, a moment or two from now, I must look back on something more meaningful than the pursuit of houses and land and stocks and bonds. Nor is fame of any lasting benefit. I will consider my earthly existence to have been wasted unless I can recall a loving family, a consistent investment in the lives of people, and an earnest attempt to serve the God who made me. Nothing else makes much sense.[1]

Dr. Dobson has a specific investment strategy for his life. You and I must also determine what is a waste of time and what is worth pursuing. That is the bottom line.

NOTES

1. James Dobson, *Straight Talk* (Waco, Tex.: Word, 1991), pp. 173–74.

8

The Dilemma of Death

Imagine reading your own obituary. Alfred Nobel had that opportunity. Around the turn of the century Nobel's brother passed away. Alfred picked up his morning paper the next day to see what was written about his brother and was stunned to discover his own obituary! The paper mistakenly printed that Alfred had died, describing him as the inventor of dynamite. Nobel realized the legacy he was leaving was associated with death and destruction.

Alfred had a second chance to rescript his legacy. With input from friends he decided to invest some of his wealth to honor those who furthered the cause of peace in the world. Today many know that Nobel invented dynamite, but he is better known for another of his creations–the Nobel Peace Prize.

You are going to leave a legacy. Your life will have a lasting impact. God has given you the capacity to think carefully about what will be left in the wake of your life and to live intentionally to leave behind something eternally worthwhile. The writer of Ecclesiastes believes that if you want to make the most of life, you must take a good long look at death. Envision your own obituary.

As a pastor I regularly get a "behind-the-scenes" glimpse of people walking through "the valley of the shadow of death." I can tell who is prepared for it, and who is not. I see families lovingly comfort one another, and I see families fighting over their share of the inheritance even before the funeral takes place. Some silently grieve the loss of a loved one; others are quietly relieved that they no longer have to deal with the person who died. Some have real hope in the face of death; others play games to convince themselves everything will be all right. Death brings out the best and the worst. And while it is not always true, I have noticed how people respond to a person's death has everything to do with how that person lived. It is part of his or her legacy.

Think carefully. Live intentionally. Take your destiny to heart.

IT'S A MATTER OF DESTINY

When you first encounter the words of Ecclesiastes 7, you might assume that the author is in a morbid mood, that he is having a really bad day. Listen to the opening words:

A good name is better than fine perfume,
  and the day of death better than the day of birth.
It is better to go to a house of mourning
  than to go to a house of feasting,
for death is the destiny of every man;
  the living should take this to heart. (7:1–2)

These last words are almost haunting: "Death is the destiny of every man; the living should take this to heart." We tend to live in denial about the reality of death. If we do think about it, we presume it is a long way off. We procrastinate forming wills and making decisions surrounding the eventuality that awaits us all. We brush aside taking our destiny to heart.

Because we are created and not the Creator, we share a destiny with the rest of God's creatures. The writer of Ecclesiastes has already considered this common destiny: "Man's fate is like that of the animals; the same fate awaits them both: As one dies, so dies the other" (3:19a). But there is a distinct difference between a human being, who has been created in the image of God, and the animals. God has "set eternity in the hearts of men" (3:11). We know death is coming, so we can live accordingly.

Coming face-to-face with your destiny is a necessary though unpleasant exercise. It will move you to make decisions you might otherwise ignore. There is an old story about a life insurance salesman who visited couples in their home. While sitting around the kitchen table, he asked the husband to get on the table and stretch out. He then pulled a sheet from his briefcase and covered him from head to toe, as they do when removing a dead body from a home. He then turned to the wife and asked, "Now what are you going to do?" I understand his antics produced some good laughs—and sold plenty of life insurance!

I must confess to a few antics myself. When I was nineteen years old and a college student, I served a church as a part-time youth pastor. During one of our youth retreats I wanted to impress on the teens the reality of death and how they should then live. I borrowed a casket from a mortician in our congregation, hauled it to the retreat location, and conducted a "funeral service." At the end of the service, I had the kids file by the casket to glimpse the "body." I had carefully placed a mirror in the casket so when they peered in, they saw their own reflection. I thought it was a great idea–about twenty-seven parents did not agree!

Little did I know they would soon come face-to-face with death in a way none of us anticipated. Steve Miller, a sixteen-year-old in the youth group, was proud of the car he had restored in his dad's body shop. Like many kids, he put in a high-powered stereo system that could cause the ground to quake. One day on his way home from school, with his stereo blasting, he failed to hear the whistle of an oncoming train as he crossed the railroad tracks–and crossed into eternity.

As our stunned youth group gathered for a meal prior to visiting the funeral home, the mood was somber. The tears were plenteous. Some life-changing decisions were made as they took death to heart.

Death is a defining moment. Taking it to heart can give definition and direction to your life. Even among Christians, whose destiny is eternal life in heaven, it is more popular to communicate a "health and wealth" gospel than a "death and suffering" gospel. While I believe we do not need to marinate in our misery, I do think we need to consider our destiny.

More people are facing that reality. Wade Clark Roof, a professor of religion at the University of California, says that as boomers enter their forties, they must face the inevitable: Neither jogging nor liposuction nor all the brown rice in China can keep them young forever. "As our bodies fall apart, as they weaken and sag, it speaks of mortality. Boomers are at a point in their lives where they sense the need for spirituality, but they don't know where to get it."[1] Awareness of the destiny of death is launching a search for the sacred.

Many men do all their preparation for living and none for dying. The tragedy is not death, but a life that is never invested or enjoyed.

> *A man may have a hundred children and live many years; yet no matter how long he lives, if he cannot enjoy his prosperity and does not receive proper burial, I say that a stillborn child is better off than he. It comes without meaning, it departs in darkness, and in darkness its name is shrouded. Though it never saw the sun or knew anything, it has more rest than does that man— even if he lives a thousand years twice over but fails to enjoy his prosperity.* (6:3–6)

A person in high school is dying to go to college. A person in college is dying to get married and begin a career. A person engulfed in career pressures is dying to retire. A person is dying—and then realizes he has never lived. Considering death is not a substitute for living, but a compass for direction in life.

Elizabeth Glaser fought a heroic battle with AIDS. Not aware that she had contracted the virus through a tainted blood transfusion, she unwittingly passed it on to her two children. One of them preceded her in death, and she feared the other would also. As she stood to say good-bye to hundreds of people gathered in the Century City Plaza Hotel in Los Angeles, she was noticeably frail:

> The great life lesson that I have consciously avoided was confronting death. I have confronted my own fears, the fears of others, social discrimination and lack of education. It has now become a time in my life to learn about and understand death. If I can do that, it will be truly an achievement.[2]

Learning about and understanding death is an achievement. The best time to learn its lessons is not when you are on your deathbed, but when you have much life ahead of you yet.

I WOULD LIKE TO OFFER THIS EULOGY

One of the defining moments of my life was preparing a eulogy for my father's funeral in the summer of 1993. My mom, sister, brother, and other family and friends had given me the raw material. It was up to me to reduce that input to a piece or two of paper, a few minutes of spoken words.

I struggled. My dad was my hero, though not because he was outwardly impressive. A man of fairly modest means and relatively few words, he was inwardly impressive. I can remember getting up in the morning and seeing him sitting on the floor next to the heat duct, an open Bible on his lap and his head bowed in thought and prayer. That picture in my mind is worth a thousand words.

My dad was a carpenter, and I worked for him to pay for college. He was the same man at work as he was at home and in church. He had consistency. He had integrity. While my personality will never be like my father's, I want his character qualities in my life.

Recently there was a conference attended by about a hundred high-powered men. These "movers-and-shakers" were being challenged to take a good, long look at their lives. The question was asked, "How many of you want to be like your dad, living life by his values and priorities?" Only about twenty hands went up. How about you? Twenty years from now, will your kids say, "I'd like to be like my dad"?

Someday one of my children may gather input from others and sit down to craft my eulogy. What pictures will come to mind? What character qualities will stand out? Will I have lived a life that is more than outwardly impressive, one that is inwardly impressive? I do not intend to leave that to chance.

In the back of my Franklin Planner I have written down my core values. They are phrased as ideals for my relationship with God, my wife, and my family, and for my personal development and my career. I have stated them as if they are already true, even though I struggle to make them a reality in my life. They are the ideals I want to live up to, and I would be honored if they were included in my eulogy someday. My life values form the eulogy I would like to offer.

You might want to pause right now. Pull out a blank sheet of paper or fire up your computer. Try to create the eulogy you would like offered at your funeral.

It might even have two parts:

Present (today): At this point in my life, what would my wife say? My kids? My coworkers? God?

Future (tomorrow): By God's grace, what might my eulogy ideally say?

Write more than an obituary, which is a brief summary of family names, achievements, organizations to which you have belonged, etc. Write a eulogy, which addresses the more personal dimensions of life. Having sat through many funerals and listened to many eulogies, it is significant to hear what is said and what is left unsaid. There is a tendency to omit weaknesses from eulogies, but in your rough draft eulogy you may want to identify them to provide opportunities for growth. It may even help to imagine yourself taking notes from your spouse, your children, and your friends. And be sure to take notes from God.

One of the most widely read and watched stories of all time is Charles Dickens' *The Christmas Carol*. The miser, Scrooge, encounters the ghost of his former business partner, who introduces him to a night of eye-opening encounters with Christmas past, Christmas present, and Christmas future. You know the story: As Scrooge glimpses the consequences of his life, he makes some choices and changes that alter forever the way he is remembered. The writer of Ecclesiastes encourages similar encounters as we take our destiny to heart.

I AM GOING TO LEAVE A LEGACY

The best time to carefully consider the legacy you will leave is after the funeral of a friend. A successful business-man in our community, who himself fought a battle with cancer that led him to alter the course of his life, served as an executor of the estate of a personal friend.

This friend was a successful attorney, who unexpect-edly died while yet in his forties. He was a committed Christian and a family man as well as a highly respected lawyer. He lived with the typical pressure of law firms, where there was an insatiable appetite for billable hours and a list of clients who would settle for no one other than him to represent their case.

The businessman shared his experience of accom-panying the attorney's wife to clean out his office a few days after the funeral. They cleared his desk and packed his per-sonal belongings. His cases had already been reassigned, another lawyer was set to move in, and this "indispensable" attorney was but a pleasant memory.

A few days of reassignment and a few files transferred completed his career. Did his impact last longer at home? Was there a greater sense of loss felt by his family and friends? Absolutely. No wonder men never say at the end of their careers that they wished they would have spent more time at the office. As the businessman executed his friend's wishes, he also developed greater wisdom about which of life's investments are lasting.

Sorrow is better than laughter,
  because a sad face is good for the heart.
The heart of the wise is in the house of mourning,
  but the heart of fools is in the house of pleasure. (7:3–4)

The wisdom necessary to focus your life's mission statement and filter the essential from the trivial will more likely come when shedding a tear than sharing a laugh. You will learn more by attending a funeral than a party.

None of us starts with a blank sheet of paper. We all have inherited the legacy of others, especially that of our parents. For some that is a great blessing, for others a cause for cursing. We are learning more as a society about the lingering effects of previous generations, but we are hardly the first to discover it. Included in the Ten Commandments is a glimpse of generational impact:

> *I, the LORD your God, am a jealous God, punishing the children for the sin of the fathers to the third and fourth generation of those who hate me, but showing love to a thousand generations of those who love me and keep my commandments.* (Exodus 20:5a–6)

It also gives us a glimpse into the gracious character of God, who limits the negative impact to a few generations while multiplying the positive impact of those who love him to a thousand generations.

As we seek to craft our eulogy and live intentionally to form a worthwhile legacy, we all carry certain baggage with us. We should be aware of the strengths of our inherited legacy that we can build on, as well as those areas by the grace of God we can rescript. Let's alternatively look at some legacy builders and some legacy breakers.

Legacy Builder #1: Heartfelt Sorrow

"A sad face is good for the heart" (7:3). Don't misunderstand—this is not an invitation to a pity party. It is a realization that there is a great deal to be learned from the grief process. Think about some of the lessons learned in the "school of loss."

Letting go. No matter how much you try and how much you cry, certain things are beyond your control. How often those who are watching a friend die painfully lament their inability to "fix it." The words "I just wish I could do something" are an admission that so little can be done beyond acts of kindness and words of comfort.

Transforming emotion into action. When the grief process begins, there is anger, guilt, doubt, fear, and sadness. As one appropriately grieves, there is a recognition that life must go on and a future be rebuilt. The overwhelming emotion slowly translates into the re-creation of a new tomorrow.

Realizing what is valuable. Grief has a winnowing effect on the priorities of life, separating the "chaff" of the urgent from the "wheat" of the important.

Sorrow provides a wonderful opportunity for life assessment. In the words of John Gardner, "To sensible men, everyday is a day of reckoning."

Legacy Breaker #1: Foolish Laughter

"Sorrow is better than laughter" (7:3). How does this square with other places in Scripture that applaud the value of laughter? For example, "A cheerful heart is good medicine, but a crushed spirit dries up the bones" (Proverbs 17:22). Medical studies demonstrate the healing effects of healthy laughter and its ability to prolong life, even in the presence of some of the deadliest diseases.

In order to understand what is being said, we must diagnose the type of laughter the author of Ecclesiastes has in mind. The clue comes a few verses later: "Like the crackling of thorns under the pot, so is the laughter of fools" (7:6). He is thinking not of the laughter of happiness, but the laughter of foolishness; not joy-filled laughter, but the nervous or rebellious laughter of one hesitant to face reality. It is the presence of a silly grin that masks the absence of a focused purpose to live life for something that outlasts it.

Legacy Builder #2: Keep the End in Sight

One of the requisites of effective leadership is the ability to maintain a disciplined focus on the purpose of an organization or cause. It is also a requisite for making the most of life. In the words of Ecclesiastes, "The end of a matter is better than its beginning" (7:8).

A lasting legacy requires disciplined choices. It will mean bypassing some opportunities for instant gratification, opting for that which provides lasting significance over a moment's pleasure. This is not to say there will not be joy in the journey or that today's emotional needs should be denied. But disciplining your emotional needs helps you to channel them into appropriate actions that provide enduring meaning for you and others.

Legacy Breaker #2: Selfish Behavior

No matter how noble a man's intentions, there are a couple of character flaws that will prevent you from obtaining the desired end: "The end of a matter is better than its beginning, and patience is better than pride" (7:8).

Pride and impatience. Pride has a way of engendering feelings of invulnerability, leading you to believe that you are on solid ground when you are really in quicksand. Rather than humbly learning life's lessons and facing death's reality, you stubbornly persist in following ingrained patterns of behavior. Pride works against patience by subtly whispering in your ear, "You deserve to have what you want — and now." This means that patiently delaying gratification in the pursuit of a higher purpose becomes nearly impossible.

Building on your strengths requires patience. Mitigating the effects of your weaknesses requires patience. Correcting significant character flaws requires patience. Upgrading the quality and intimacy of your relationships requires patience. Patience is a legacy builder, while pride is a legacy breaker.

The Teacher flags a second common destroyer of a worthwhile legacy: anger. "Do not be quickly provoked in your spirit, for anger resides in the lap of fools" (7:9). This volcanic force causes many to forfeit their long-term positive influence. When you are angry, you say things you do not mean to say and do things you do not mean to do. Many men have high aspirations for their relationships with their families, yet those aspirations for a legacy of love are overridden in the minds of those they care for by memories of physical, emotional, or verbal abuse.

Being "quickly provoked" is often triggered not by what is going on around you, but by what is going on inside of you. Many men have been deeply hurt and carry a load of shame that seems unbearable. But it is not macho to admit that you are hurting or that you have been shamed unfairly. We are taught to deny we are struggling with anger. So a man goes on exploding at others, when what he would really like to do is sit with his head in his hands and cry like a baby.

I will never forget the struggle one man shared with me. He had been hurt and shamed by his father's perfectionist tendencies and legalistic religion. In an atmosphere of conditional paternal love, he grew up stuffing his frustration inside until its volatility could no longer be contained. At his father's funeral he felt numb, unable to grieve his death. He buried the pain of the moment in "fixing" the feelings of others who mourned his father's loss.

Several years later, his own life increasingly in shambles due to unresolved hurt and shame, he felt trapped in his anger. He could not confront a father who was dead or be reconciled to him. He decided to drive to his father's grave in another state, and there in the cemetery he vented his feelings. He ranted, then he cried, and then by the grace of God he forgave. His honesty about his woundedness, along with the healing grace of God, was a new beginning. He was free to rescript his legacy.

Pride and anger are not conquered in your own strength. God's Spirit can free your spirit from their tenacious grip. But often that grip is loosened little by little. Patiently pursuing a character change is made possible by God as you honestly face your dilemma and humbly seek his intervention.

Legacy Builder #3: Reinforcing Relationships

Building a lasting legacy is a process of aligning your purposes with God's purposes. That can only be done in his strength and through a disciplined focus in your life's choices. You cannot go it alone, however; you need the encouragement of others who know the desired end and provide positive peer pressure to live for it. You undoubtedly know the people who will reinforce your will power to live for life's highest purposes. And you can also identify those who will distract you from your desired legacy.

For me, my appointment with my accountability partner every other week is a legacy builder. During that time I review my "Top Ten" list of goals. These goals are little and measurable steps. When consistently met over time, they move me toward my desired "end of the matter." This session also gives me an opportunity to share my struggles and get the encouragement I need to stay the course. Because I am a guy who needs more help than most (my wife will attest to this), I also meet with a small group of men, known as the Iron Men ("As iron sharpens iron, so one man sharpens another"–Proverbs 27:17). They strengthen my resolve to live for things of lasting significance. We attempt through the books we read and the prayer requests we share to develop a "top of the line" eternal perspective, then live for it.

Who reinforces your willpower? Who prays for you and your life's purposes on a regular basis? These men are your legacy builders. I am convinced you will naturally encounter those who will distract you. I am also convinced you must intentionally seek out partners and mentors to walk with you and keep you on track. In the words of comedian Tim Allen, "All men like to think they can do it alone, but a real man knows there's no substitute for support, encouragement, or a pit crew."

Legacy Breaker #3: The Good Old Days

A "legacy mentality" is a future focus. Developing a life mission statement sets the path of your tomorrows. It is dangerous to move forward while looking backward. "Do not say, 'Why were the old days better than these?' For it is not wise to ask such questions" (7:10). Ah, those good old days—reminiscing about the days gone by. Many people not only dwell on them, they live in them. They back into the future.

This does not mean you should not celebrate your successes. I, like most men, tend to accomplish something and immediately ask, "What's next?" Looking back with satisfaction to see a trail of steps that move us ahead toward our desired future is not only admirable, it is a motivator. A healthy look back turbocharges the continued pursuit of your life's mission.

If you pin people down concerning what was better about the old days, invariably they mention that people were not as busy then. There was more time for relationships, and these relationships lasted longer. But you can have the best of the good old days without reverting back to them. Build into your life mission time to relax and time to develop relationships. It will not happen naturally or easily, but it can happen. Then you have the best of both worlds—present-day opportunities to pursue your future dreams with the "old day" qualities that helped press meaning into life.

A final word about legacy-building. A balancing act between two views is essential. Some men view themselves as trapped in their past, victims of their inherited legacy. This view is especially prevalent among men who have grown up in abusive or alcoholic homes. They feel their future can only be an extension of their past. It is admirable, of course, to grieve legitimately the downside of your inherited legacy and accept the reality of the hand dealt to you. But never underestimate God's grace not only to provide forgiveness for your past and heal its hurts, but also to empower you to rescript your future.

The other extreme is the view that "I am master of my destiny." It hallucinates that all that will be included in one's legacy lies within one's control. Instead, proper goals and actions are "Lego blocks" in the hands of God. When you have done your part, you must realize ultimately that he assembles the building blocks of your efforts into a design for his purposes.

IT JUST KEEPS GOING AND GOING

Gary Thomas argues that "Wise Christians Clip Obituaries." One of his clippings includes the funeral of one of the world's most powerful leaders:

> As Vice President, George Bush represented the United States at the funeral of former Soviet leader Leonid Brezhnev. Bush was deeply moved by a silent protest carried out by Brezhnev's widow. She stood motionless by the coffin until seconds before it was closed. Then, just as the soldiers touched the lid, Brezhnev's wife performed an act of great courage and hope, a gesture that must surely rank as one of the most profound acts of civil disobedience ever committed: She reached down and made the sign of the cross on her husband's chest.

There, in the citadel of secular, atheistic power, the wife of the man who had run it all hoped that her husband was wrong. She hoped that there was another life, and that life was best represented by Jesus who died on the cross, and that the same Jesus might yet have mercy on her husband.[3]

A legacy without preparation for eternity is an act of futility. Someone using their finger to outline a cross on the chest of our corpse will not make an eternal difference for us. You and I must decide for ourselves to take up our cross and follow him. We must repent of our selfish attempts to orchestrate life to fulfill only our own desires. We must build a lasting legacy with eternal consequence through following Jesus. Following him is what forms a spiritual, eternal legacy.

Make no mistake about what offers hope in the face of eternity. One religious man I know estimated his good works would be enough. He figured that on a scale of one to ten, he was a seven. He concluded that if God grades on a curve, he was in. He would make the cut. Then he came face-to-face with cancer. He suddenly became serious about where hope is really found—in forgiveness through Jesus Christ and a willingness to respond to his Lordship.

Some men make the mistake of never considering what their eulogy will be. Their lives are like a walk on the seashore, where the waves wash their footprints away. Others live so that people will say nice things about them, having never discovered that there is a difference between simply pleasing people and really loving people. Ultimately, the best eulogies have one's relationship with God interwoven with every other relationship and achievement in life. So ask yourself:

What will rise to the surface at your death?

Are you willing to rescript? What stands in the way?

Who are the people who are your legacy-builders? legacy-breakers?

Have you begun work on a life mission statement, an intentional design for your personal legacy?

Begin today. Don't get discouraged by trying to construct the perfect mission statement, the most eloquent eulogy. It is a "work in progress." Add to it. Subtract from it. In the sentiments of Peter Drucker, "Plans are nothing. Planning is everything." It is not what ultimately lands on a piece of paper that counts; it is what you learned in the process that really matters.

Max Lucado, one of my favorite authors, shares this story:

> I recently read an insightful story that would serve as a good reminder for us both as we prepare to part ways. The story is about a group of climbers who set out to scale a large mountain in Europe. The view boasted a breathtaking peak of snowcapped rocks. On clear days the crested point reigned as king on the horizon. Its white tip jutted into the blue sky inviting admiration and offering inspiration.
>
> On days like this the hikers made the greatest progress. The peak stood above them like a compelling goal. Eyes were called upward. The walk was brisk. The cooperation was unselfish. Though many, they climbed as one, all looking to the same summit.
>
> Yet on some days the peak of the mountain was hidden from view. The cloud covering would eclipse the crisp blueness with a drab, gray ceiling and block the vision of the mountaintop. On these days the climb became arduous. Eyes were downward and thoughts inward. The goal

THE DILEMMA OF DEATH

was forgotten. Tempers were short. Weariness was an uninvited companion. Complaints stung like thorns on the trail.

We're like that, aren't we? As long as we can see our dream, as long as our goal is within eyesight, there is no mountain we can't climb or summit we can't scale. But take away our vision, block our view of the trail's end, and the result is as discouraging as the journey.[4]

Don't lose sight of your ultimate goal, the peak of eternity—a lasting legacy. Keep climbing!

NOTES

1. *Newsweek* (November 28, 1994).

2. *People* (December 19, 1994).

3. *Christianity Today* (October 3, 1994).

4. Max Lucado, *God Came Near* (Portland, Ore: Multnomah, 1987), p. 160.

9

Don't Lose Your Balance

SCRIPTURE: ECCLESIASTES 7:13–20

We live in a world that exalts people who give everything they have to be the best in one dimension of life. Headlines go to the athlete who sacrifices everything to finish on top of his game. A partnership is awarded to the workaholic who relentlessly piles up billable hours. Promotions are granted to the executive who will move anywhere and anytime to grasp the next rung on the corporate ladder.

Not only are these single-minded pursuits applauded, but they are a way of living toward which bottom-line men are naturally inclined. A strength common among us is the ability to focus our lives to accomplish a desired purpose. But an overextension of a strength can become a weakness. It is possible to be too focused, or as Bob Buford coins it, to "hyper-focus." You can become so intent on accomplishment in one area of life that you neglect other equally important dimensions of life.

God's "top of the line" view of excellence is on a collision course with the one-dimensional life. While you may not read about "balanced life" awards in *Sports Illustrated* or *Forbes*, the Bible honors a balanced life. It is a powerful test of your trust in God. Do you believe you can live a balanced life and still be successful? Is God capable of granting you that desired promotion even if you do not work seventy hours a week? Is God able to give you a wonderful relationship with your children even if you do not cater to their every desire?

Life is a balancing act. Do not lose your balance. Grasp career opportunities, but do not neglect your marriage. Make time for your children, but do not forfeit all of your time for serving God and others. Build a diversified portfolio of life investment.

What is balance from God's perspective? Do not confuse God's call to the "balanced best" with common misconceptions:

1. *Balance is not an excuse for mediocrity or apathy.* God calls you to do your best in relationships and accomplishments. Do not cultivate a balanced life by developing an "I don't care" attitude. Pursuing balance does not mean caring less about areas of life in which you might go overboard. It is learning to care more deeply and intensely about areas you might neglect. If you tend to focus on your job and neglect your wife, the answer is not convincing yourself to be satisfied with mediocrity in the workplace. It is to think and focus more intentionally on the home front.

2. *Balance is not a cover for control.* It is not a front for selfishly pursuing your own agenda. Sometimes the needs of your family, the hurts of a friend, or the demands of your employer may affect your plan for balanced living. For me as a

pastor, a balanced life means observing a day off, a regular release from the routine of responding to people's needs. But my commitment to a day off should not prevent me from responding to the occasional legitimate crisis that may arise on that day. Balance must be somewhat fluid, not selfishly rigid.

3. *Balance is not a spiritual "ideal state."* It is not a form of the illusory nirvana. We tend to think other men's lives are more balanced than ours. We tend to believe if we were only more "spiritual," we would have better balance in life. In reality, balance is always being pursued. Life is always throwing you off balance. Like a car tire, the natural tendency is to get out of balance. You may not be aware of it until you begin to notice signs of wear and tear. Realigning life when it gets out of balance is a continual process.

What is God's description of a balanced life? Most often it is envisioned as a prioritization process—giving the various dimensions of life their proper place. It raises questions like, "How do I juggle work and family responsibilities? How do I spend, save, and give the appropriate amounts of money?" These are important questions.

The writer of Ecclesiastes, however, takes the pursuit of God's balanced best a step further. He helps you confront dilemmas such as:

- In any endeavor, what is God's part (which he alone can do) and what is my part?
- How do I make the most of life in good times and in tough times?
- How can I be "heavenly-minded," yet well-grounded in this day-to-day world?

Let's examine more closely what his journal has to say.

GOD'S PART/YOUR PART

Consider what God has done:
Who can straighten
 what he has made crooked? (7:13)

Living life to the fullest is a matter of trusting and trying. You must trust God to do what only he can do. You must then try to do what he expects of you. That means discerning God's part and your part. You are responsible for your part, nothing more and nothing less. Then you must trust God to bring about his desired outcome.

I wish I could give you a simple formula for identifying your part and God's part. Theologians describe it as the balance between God's sovereignty and human responsibility, and no two theologians see it in the same way! God does not always choose to act predictably. If he did, you could control his actions. You would know that if you do "A" and "B," God will always do "C." In reality, you may do "A" and "B," but then God decides it is in your best interest to experience "M." You can try to convince him to act otherwise. And you will likely conclude, "Who can straighten out what he has made crooked?"

Only God can straighten out what he has made crooked. God determines when he will place a crook in the path, a curve in life's road. The writer of Ecclesiastes invites us to "consider what God has done." Why does God choose to make things crooked?

Picture for a moment some possibilities:

1. Think of a path with a turn in it. If the path is always straight, then you are always headed in the same direction. The "crook in the road" may be God's way of redirecting the focus of your life.

2. Envision a maze. At a fun center in our area kids can run through a maze while the parents watch from above. When you are in the maze, the twists and turns are puzzling. From above, the way out is clear. The one in the maze has a much more limited perspective. God may be demonstrating the limits of your vision, leading you to rely more completely on his heavenly vantage point.

3. Imagine a golf course winding through the woods. It would be easier if every hole were a straight line from tee to cup (unless you have a slice like mine!). It is the obstacles and variations that make the course interesting. God may be adding "interest" to your life!

4. Picture a race track with hairpin curves. On the straightaway drivers pick up speed; on the turns they slow down and exercise additional caution. Maybe God is seeking to slow you down or get your attention.

Other pictures may come to your mind. The invitation is not to figure God out, but to consider his ways. We must do our part, and God will do his part–and he will not always do what we predict.

This is not to say God is completely unpredictable! The promises of his Word assure you of predictable responses to certain actions. For instance, "If we confess our sins, he is faithful and just and will forgive us our sins and purify us from all unrighteousness" (1 John 1:9). If you do your part (genuinely confess), God will do his part (forgive). Not half the time. Not nine times out of ten. But every time! You can count on it. God is predictable in his overall plan of redemption.

Yet he remains unpredictable as to how specific events will work out in your life. Derek Kidner is right when he says, "The mystery of what God sends, and especially the unpredictability of it, clips the wings of our self-sufficiency."

Often your part will be a choice—rebellion or cooperation? Will you resist God's decisions or respond to his sometimes mysterious purpose for your life? Larry Crabb tells this story about the unexpected death of his brother. When asked, "How did that affect your understanding of God's love?" he wrote:

> Bill's death made absolutely no sense. After drifting in his spiritual life, he had recommitted himself to God more than 20 years before he died. And he still had so much more to give to his wife and children.
>
> Losing Bill shocked us all. My dad was 78 at the time. When he got word of the crash, he went outside and screamed at God for ten minutes. And then, he told me later, "When God wouldn't repent, I had to trust him."
>
> Hearing my dad say he trusted God even when he wouldn't "repent" helped me think through one of the core issues of my faith. Of course God didn't repent. What does he have to repent of? He never makes a mistake.
>
> In the midst of my questioning and my bouts of despair, I still believe in God. I believe he made himself known in his Son. And I believe that when I look at the cross I get the clearest picture of the character and the heart of God. His character is he hates sin, and his nature is he loves sinners. Those are the bottom-line issues.[1]

Have you ever, like Larry's father, tried to get God to repent? I have. God lovingly reminds me that he is not the one who needs to change, I do. He challenges us to trust him.

There is a paradox in Scripture. The God who makes things crooked is fully capable of making our paths straight. One example of this promise is given is in Proverbs: "He will make your paths straight." But there is a prerequisite to that promise:

Trust in the Lord with all your heart
and lean not on your own understanding;
in all your ways acknowledge him,
and he will make your paths straight. (Proverbs 3:5–6)

Notice the order. It is not, "God, you make my paths straight so I know clearly the direction of my life; then I will trust you." No, the order is, "I trust, straight or crooked, and then he will straighten the path to pursue his purposes for my life."

These realities do not diminish the value of planning, but they do emphasize the importance of discerning between God's part and your part. The process of planning leads you to anticipate the future, though your exact plans may never materialize. You should plan and pursue these plans, for "God cannot steer a parked car." But do not fixate on those plans; stay flexible. As James expresses it:

> *Now listen, you who say, "Today or tomorrow*
> *we will go to this or that city, spend a year there,*
> *carry on business and make money." Why, you do*
> *not even know what will happen tomorrow. What*
> *is your life? You are a mist that appears for a*
> *while and then vanishes. Instead, you ought to*
> *say, "If it is the Lord's will, we will live and do this*
> *or that." As it is, you boast and brag. All such*
> *boasting is evil.* (James 4:13–16)

Planning is beneficial; presumption is hazardous. The difference is found in carefully doing your part while humbly submitting to God's larger purposes for your life.

GOOD TIMES/BAD TIMES

The author of Ecclesiastes pushes our thinking a bit further. "When times are good, be happy" (7:14a). Make the most of them. Don't feel guilty about good times or fail to celebrate the positive experiences of life. "But when times are bad, consider: God has made one as well as the other" (7:14b). His recommended response to good times? Enjoy them! His recommended response to bad times? They are good food for thought. They provide an opportunity to remember that God is Creator of both good and bad experiences in life.

The Bible makes it clear that not all bad experiences are authored by God. Bad things happen when a man violates God's design; that reality goes back all the way to Adam, whose "fling with the fruit" opened the door for untold sin, suffering, and death. So sometimes you will experience disappointment, even tragedy, as a consequence of resisting God's will and being disobedient to his plan.

Bad things also occur when others violate God's design for their lives and we pay the price. The consequences of another person's sinfulness may impact you deeply. A parent in uncontrolled anger abuses his or her child emotionally or physically, deeply scarring that child's spirit. An employer is a poor steward of company resources and causes a man to lose his job. A stockbroker unethically or ineptly manages a retiree's portfolio, and a lifetime of savings is lost.

This is not to say God is helpless in these situations, even though they do not reflect his will. God is miraculously capable of redeeming even the most devastating violations of his design. Remember Joseph? His brothers, in a fit of jealousy and rage, sold him as a young teenager to a passing caravan of Midianites. He spent years in slavery and in prison before God placed him in a strategic leadership position. Toward the end of his life, Joseph was able to say to his brothers, "Don't be afraid. Am I in the place of God? You intended to harm me, but God intended it for good to accomplish what is now being done, the saving of many lives" (Genesis 50:19–20). God created a life mission from the ashes of life's devastation.

So God is not the maker of all negative circumstances. Nonetheless, he is the maker of both the good times and the bad. Your good times and your bad times are authored by God, edited by God, or permitted by God. He is able to create the perfect recipe of good and bad ingredients that accomplish his purpose for your life. He knows exactly how much you can handle comfortably. No, not comfortably. He knows exactly how much you can manage *productively* in your life. While God is sensitive to your comfort level, he will risk extending your comfort zones to produce his character in you.

God is committed to developing 100 percent of your potential. While in theory that sounds inspiring, in practice it can be intimidating. To develop that potential he uses both good and bad. Many times I have attempted to negotiate with God, letting him know I would gladly settle for 90 percent of my potential if he will let me pass on some of life's hardest lessons. He gently reminds me that he loves me, that he is monitoring my "vital signs" personally and spiritually, but that he uses a balance of positive and negative to bring about 100 percent of his purpose for me.

You may have trouble accepting "good times" from God. You naturally feel unworthy, unable fully to receive his blessings. More likely you will have trouble accepting "bad times" from God. Maturity comes in processing both and incorporating the benefits of both into your life. That requires a "top of the line" flexibility, a divine elasticity in life.

Here are some practices for processing the bad times:

1. Have a conversation (or confrontation) with God. Sometimes he is the last one we consider talking to. Conduct that conversation through prayer, reading his Word, and jotting some notes in your journal. Attempt to envision what God is up to, developing your understanding of his perspective. In the words of Larry Crabb, "I believe a central theme of the Christian life is that we shouldn't use God to solve our problems. Instead, we should see our problems as an opportunity to find God. Doing everything you can to relieve the hurt doesn't address the source of the pain."[2]

2. Surround yourself with encouraging people—not just men who will join your pity party, but those who will reinforce your capacity to sense God's love and discover his purpose in difficult times.

3. Fix your eyes on Jesus. In a world where corporations are discovering that one key to a successful future is strategic focus, we need to discover the power of Jesus' example. His willingness to endure the ultimate form of suffering inspires us to ultimate allegiance to God, even when we feel (as he did), "My God, my God, why have you forsaken me?" (Matthew 27:46).

One of the reasons the gospel is "good news" is the incurable, or should I say, eternal optimism it generates for all the experiences of life.

God is the maker of both good times and bad times, but what about the in-between times? They seem to be the "no man's land." Life is not that good, but not that bad either. It is easy to get restless during these times when you feel like God is riding the fence. You are not taking three steps forward or two steps back. You feel as if you are standing still. It is still beneficial to seek God's perspective, surround yourself with encouragers, and focus your attention on Jesus. In fact, you can benefit from these practices whether in good times, bad times, or the neutral times of life.

A LIFE OF BALANCE

A life of balance is a demonstration of reverence for God.

Do not be overrighteous,
neither be overwise—
why destroy yourself?
Do not be overwicked,
and do not be a fool—
why die before your time?
It is good to grasp the one
and not let go of the other.
The man who fears God will avoid all extremes.

(7:16–18)

He is speaking the language of balance: "Avoid extremes." In the process of pursuing one priority in life, do "not let go of the other."

Do Not Be Overrighteous

While balance is important in all of life, the writer of Ecclesiastes highlights its special importance in spiritual life: "Do not be overrighteous." There are many men whose legitimate passion for a righteous cause has degenerated into legalism and self-righteousness. This is especially true when they believe they have a special knowledge in that area. "Neither be overwise." It is heresy to take one dimension of God's truth and overemphasize it until it occupies a place in one's thinking that God never intended.

I have seen men whose love for God has generated a righteous concern. Worthy causes include family values, sanctity of life, living debt-free, and boycotting certain companies. Over time, however, that "cause" takes the central place in their lives and Christ is marginalized. Christ becomes a means to an end. He is seen as the source of power to do what you feel strongly about rather than the person who transforms and takes control of your life. Passion for a cause and knowledge of the issue inflate your self-importance and negate your love for God. The apostle Paul, writing to a church embroiled in a heated debate over an issue that generated strong convictions, said:

> *We know that we all possess knowledge.*
> *Knowledge puffs up, but love builds up. The man*
> *who thinks he knows something does not yet know*
> *as he ought to know. But the man who loves God*
> *is known by God.* (1 Corinthians 8:1–3)

Paul reminds us that while knowledge and conviction are worth grasping, we should never let go of loving God and being known by God.

Recently a group of college students were given a list of words and asked to select the one they most associated with Christianity. Seven out of eight indicated the word that most predominantly came to their minds was "bigotry." Granted, this survey was conducted in Washington D.C., and the media has significantly distorted reality in its portrayal of Christian concerns. But does it also indicate that many Christians have wandered from "loving God and being known by God" to "loving a cause and knowing all you can about it"?

Do Not Be Overwicked

An even greater problem exists on the other side of the continuum. "Do not be overwicked and do not be a fool." Things have degenerated so completely that it is no longer just the church or Promise Keepers that is sounding the alarm. A recent *Newsweek* cover reads: "Shame: How Do We Bring Back a Sense of Right and Wrong?"[3] An inside article boldly asks, "What Ever Happened to Sin?" In an era when sin is barely mentioned in churches, a secular magazine is waving the banner!

One day after completing my workout, I paused in front of a large screen TV at the club. The *Today* show was interviewing a sociologist discussing the impact of talk shows on our culture. She shrewdly observed that these shows were precipitating the "numbing and dumbing" of America. Guests on the shows were "confusing fame with shame." She lamented that by glamorizing aberrant behavior, we were lowering the threshold of morality. In the words of Ecclesiastes, being "overwicked" and "a fool."

How do you attain the balance between "over-righteousness" and "overwickedness" that demonstrates reverence for God?

1. Let nothing assume central place in your heart other than your allegiance to Christ. No cause, however necessary or worthy, should take his seat of lordship in your life. The gospel is good news of spiritual transformation through the redemptive work of Jesus Christ. No other agenda should take precedence over God's agenda to transform your life and eternal destiny.

2. Opposites are attractive in pursuing balance. If you are a Christian, you are in the world (an everyday existence "beneath the sun") but not of the world (your ultimate purpose is directed "above the sun"). You are to be a leader (grasp the influence God seeks to give you) but also a servant (not lose sight of the needs of others). You are to hate sin (strongly reject that which is a violation of God's design) but love the sinner (God demonstrated his love for us by sending Christ to die for us "while we were still sinners," Romans 5:8).

In a nutshell, you are to strive for righteousness but never forget your weakness. You are to pursue purity in a spirit of humility.

Extremism is an enemy of the balanced spiritual life God intends for you to live. But it is not the only enemy. Many men lose their balance because of another one: perfectionism. People drive themselves with unrealistic expectations they can never meet. They rarely comprehend the valuable lessons of life learned only in the school of failure.

Perfectionism causes you to turn inward and "beat yourself up" over your inability to meet God's standards or your own ideals. It generates a fear of moving beyond your comfort zones and taking new risks because you might fail. It causes you to procrastinate the completion of projects, because as long as those projects are "in process," you do not have to admit their imperfection. It can poison relationships with a lack of grace. Ecclesiastes says that nobody is perfect: "There is not a righteous man on earth who does what is right and never sins" (7:20).

One of the protections against becoming over-righteous is the recognition you can never be completely righteous. This does not mean you should give up on the cause of righteousness any more than your inability to be a perfect father should cause you to give up on father-hood. But it should motivate you to seek what only God can provide:

- Forgiveness when you fail to honor God and others
- Wisdom to redeem the consequences of wrong choices
- Strength to begin again so that failure is not final.

Do Not Be Overly Sensitive

Being overly sensitive to your critics is third enemy of spiritual balance:

Do not pay attention to every word people say,
  or you may hear your servant cursing you—
for you know in your heart
  that many times you have cursed others. (7:21–22)

Criticizing and cursing others has become a national pastime. It is symptomatic of the overall cynicism of our day. The greater your influence as a leader, the bigger the target you become for others. The writer of Ecclesiastes reminds you that just as "nobody is perfect," so "you will never please everyone." As John Maxwell says, "I can't give you a formula for success, but I can give you a formula for failure. Try to please everyone." Trying to please everyone causes life to spin out of control.

The apostle Paul was effective in reaching out to people. Yet he had his strong critics. While sensitive to the perceptions of others, the compass of his life was set on God's perception of him.

We are not trying to please men but God, who tests our hearts. You know we never used flattery, nor did we put on a mask to cover up greed—God is our witness. We were not looking for praise from men, not from you or anyone else. (1 Thessalonians 2:4–6)

This attitude did not diminish his concern for others. It expressed his refusal to allow the agenda of his life to be determined by the compliments and criticisms of others.

There is a world of difference between "pleasing people" and "loving people." When you are pleasing people, you are constantly trying to figure out what they want and scrambling to provide it for them. Any hope for a balanced life is lost in the frantic attempt to satiate their growing and changing desires. When you are loving people, you are seeking what God wants for them and trying to do your part in providing what they truly need.

PURSUING GOD'S BALANCED BEST

Finding balance in life may seem elusive. What should you do when things are out of balance?

1. Get back to the basics. Uncomplicate life. Take one day at a time. Get up in the morning with a determination to love God, to love your family and friends, and to be diligent in focusing on your primary responsibilities.

2. Try to sort out your part from God's part. In the words of Ecclesiastes:

   All this I tested by wisdom and I said,
   "I am determined to be wise"—

but this was beyond me.
Whatever wisdom may be,
  it is far off and most profound—
  who can discover it? ...
This only have I found:
  God made mankind upright,
  but men have gone in search of many schemes.
(7:23–24, 29)

Don't try to scheme your way out of the situation. Ask God what he expects you to do and trust him to do what you cannot.

3. Ask God the right questions. Don't constantly ask, "What did I do wrong?" but ask, "What is God saying to me in this situation?" There may be wrongs that need to be made right, and if you are listening, God will let you know. Perhaps you have done nothing wrong, but God has placed you in the learning laboratory of life in which a lack of balance is raising the need for some necessary realignment.
4. Seek the help of a friend or accountability partner. Loss of balance often results from unaddressed blind spots. The early warning signals of a friend can spare you unnecessary wear and tear from a life out of balance.

NOTES

1. Larry Crabb, "Do You Ever Suspect God Isn't Good?" *Marriage Partnership* (Spring 1995), p. 63.

2. Ibid., p. 51.

3. *Newsweek* (February 2, 1995).

10

Which Race Are You Running?

SCRIPTURE: ECCLESIASTES 10:1–14

I am a "hobby" runner. You have heard of hobby farmers—people who dabble in farming but don't work the farm as if their livelihood depended on it. That is my attitude toward running—I dabble in it only for its cardiovascular benefits. I run about ten miles a week, five hundred miles a year. I clip along at about an eight-minute-a-mile pace.

I have dreamed about doing marathons, but have only trained for five-kilometer races. I have learned a few things along the way:

- The faster you seek to run, the greater the commitment. If I want to shave just one minute a mile off my time, substantial effort is required.
- The longer the race, the greater the training required. You may be able to run a mile without training, but probably not five miles, and certainly not ten.

- The race you run determines how you prepare and the strategy you use. The hundred-yard sprint mandates a completely different training regimen and strategy than a marathon.

Life is a marathon. Many men begin their lives at a sprint, fooled by the fast pace of our society. They may use drugs to keep the pace—everything from cocaine to caffeine. Or they may run on their own adrenaline. Exhausted after their initial sprint, they realize there is so much life yet ahead—the best years of their lives, if they are willing to change strategies.

Which race are you running? You must choose your personal paradigm. Will you be a sprinter who makes a short-term difference, or will you be a marathoner who lives a life of long-term effectiveness? You must decide; it cannot be left to chance. If you do not decide, someone or something else will make the decision for you. Picture how you want to run and finish your life's race. Make decisions today—and every day—to work toward that picture.

The tendency is to lose the marathon perspective. We live in a world that desperately needs marathoners—marathon marriages, marathon ministries, marathon men. The challenge of the marathon is the change in terrain. Sprints are run on a level surface, but marathons have hills and valleys, uphills and downhills, the wind at your back and the wind in your face. It requires a strategy for the variety of terrain you encounter in the course of the race.

My dad was a builder for many decades, and in his career he saw many construction companies come and go. The construction business, like many others, is cyclical. Many men whose business flourished in the upswing of the cycle floundered in the downswing. A marathoner learns to run well in all the "cycles" of life—when the leg muscles are screaming on the uphill or stretching on the downhill.

Life is a marathon. At times you may need to run faster or slower, to exert more energy or conserve your energy, to persevere in an uphill segment or cruise along in a downhill segment. The writer of Ecclesiastes shares his insights for long-term effectiveness. I call them "Memos to Marathoners."

MEMOS TO MARATHONERS

Memo #1: "Let's Be Careful Out There"

A popular television show for many years, *Hill Street Blues*, always began with a briefing for the police officers before they hit the streets. They learned the events that had happened since their last shift, things to watch out for, and precautions to take. The briefing always ended with the sergeant saying, "Hey! Hey! Hey! Let's be careful out there!" It was his way of reminding them that a moment of carelessness could have dire consequences.

The writer of Ecclesiastes issues a similar warning that has a ring of familiarity to it. You may have heard the statement, "There's a fly in the ointment." His warning is a modified version: "As dead flies give perfume a bad smell, so a little folly outweighs wisdom and honor" (10:1). An apothecary in his day would carefully select spices from his shelf, creating a recipe for the scent he desired. He carefully mixed those spices together into an extract and then combined that extract with oil. That mixture was then placed in a pot to age. If, in a moment of carelessness, he or his assistant failed to cover the jar and a fly fell in, the batch was spoiled. The errant path of one fly ruined hours of effort and creativity.

SOUL MANAGEMENT

Several years ago my wife and I visited an area restaurant. As we enjoyed a salad before our entree, she discovered, floating in the dressing in the bottom of her salad bowl, a foreign object—a dead fly. Needless to say, that ruined her appetite. We have not been back to that restaurant for a meal together since. When she recently ate there with a friend, I was surprised. But she made it clear she did not order the salad! A fine restaurant, but a moment's carelessness devastated its reputation in our minds.

While I was writing this chapter, Gary Moeller, long-term football coach of the University of Michigan, was arrested for a night of drunken revelry. His assistant coach, Lloyd Carr, lamented his downfall in the *Detroit Free Press*:

> Everyone wants to make sense of it, but how many rational things do people do who have had too much to drink? A man, in the space of a week, has all the things he's worked for taken away. I don't know a man who worked harder and cared more about kids than that man.[1]

As the article summarized it, "On one night [Moeller] did the highly unexpected, and none of what he'd done on the previous 8000-plus days as a U of M employee seemed to matter anymore." The headline across the page was entitled, "Who's Next?"

"A little folly outweighs wisdom and honor." It is far easier to ruin something than to create it. A single reckless moment can undo years of honor. Folly carries more weight than wisdom and honor. The scales tip toward carelessness.

Song of Songs is a book of the Bible from which you may never hear a sermon series. It is the record of an intimate dialogue between two lovers—presumably husband

and wife. It gets quite graphic as they discuss their appreciation for each other physically and emotionally. Tucked into this lovers' conversation are some great tidbits of wisdom, expressed in poetic language. Here is one: "Catch for us the foxes, our little foxes that ruin the vineyards, the vineyards that are in bloom" (Song of Songs 2:15). This is an image of the little things (pictured as "foxes") that tear up a growing relationship (pictured as a "vineyard"). Minor irritants, trivial in and of themselves individually, combine to threaten a relationship. A married couple wisely seeks to contain them before they can do their damage.

When men experience some success, they often begin to feel invulnerable. It is easy to assume arrogantly that their accomplishments have happened because of their efforts (it may have happened in spite of them!). That feeling of invulnerability is the forerunner of stupidity! In the words of the apostle Paul, "So, if you think you are standing firm, be careful that you don't fall!" (1 Corinthians 10:12). When you begin to take credit for what God has done, you begin to assume mistakenly that you do not have to play by the rules anymore. Satan whispers in your ear that little "indiscretions" will not matter. Just a quick drink after work with that female coworker—your wife doesn't even have to know. Just a slight misrepresentation on your tax form—the government wastes money anyway. Just a little distortion on your expense form—your salary is lower than what you deserve. Such statements are reminiscent of another impression left in a garden a long time ago: "It's just a little piece of fruit—go ahead and try it!" A moment of carelessness sets the course of destruction.

The writer of Ecclesiastes expresses the danger of carelessness another way: "The heart of the wise inclines to the right, but the heart of the fool to the left" (10:2). This is not a political statement or a slam against left-handers

(I could take it personally; though I am left-handed, I want to be right-hearted!). It is a biblical way of saying that wisdom carefully chooses the best in life.

In the language of Wisdom Literature, the right hand was associated with greater blessings. While the left may represent something that is good, the right represents what is best. It takes great wisdom to select from among good opportunities the best. Sometimes carelessness is manifested as a pattern of choosing less than the best. Because life is in many ways the sum total of the decisions we make, our choices have a cumulative effect.

Along the shore of Lake Michigan was a cross-country course that was not as clearly marked as it should have been. As a result, the lead runners ended up choosing the wrong direction and ended up nowhere near the finish line. The slower runners observed the markers and stayed the course. The fastest runners did not win that day. No amount of speed could compensate for missing the markers!

The greater the distance, the greater the difference a little variance can make. Imagine scientists preparing to launch a rocket that is tilted just one or two degrees off course. While unnoticeable to the untrained eye, a single degree can result in being a million miles off course as the rocket travels further into space. The trajectory that results from slight misdirection may be so far off the mark that a mid-course correction becomes nearly impossible.

You must cautiously choose the best, that is, you must incline to the right. We all will require mid-course corrections, and God graciously grants us those opportunities. But a consistent pattern of discerning the best helps us stay the course of marathon effectiveness.

If carelessness is causing you to feel less vulnerable, remember foolishness outweighs all that your wisdom may have brought to you. If carelessness is causing you to choose the less valuable, incline your heart again in the direction of lasting blessings. Let's be careful out there!

Memo #2: "Don't Bite the Hand That Feeds You"

So much of our capacity to be marathoners relates to our response to authority: the authority of God, the authority of those to whom we are accountable, and even our own authority. Many men have forfeited long-term effectiveness by thoughtlessness in responding to unjust treatment.

If a ruler's anger rises against you,
do not leave your post;
calmness can lay great errors to rest. (10:4)

If your boss gets angry and wrongly takes it out on you, don't make matters worse by responding in a way you will regret later. This is especially tough if your boss is not only angry, but incompetent.

There is an evil I have seen under the sun,
the sort of error that arises from a ruler:
Fools are put in many high positions,
while the rich occupy the low ones.
I have seen slaves on horseback,
while princes go on foot like slaves. (10:5–7)

It is uncanny to see the number of people who are promoted to one level above their competency. It may even be true of us! There is frequently a mismatch between a man's position and a man's performance. Positional authority can never take the place of credibility, whether the person is a parent, a boss, or a spiritual leader.

Never let another person's action determine your reaction. Make your choices in life related to God's direction and your decisions. Do not forfeit your responsibility to calmly pursue the best in life. So many potential marathoners blame their failure to stay the course on the thoughtless action of others.

From time to time I bump into a man who has left his career, attributing it to a "matter of principle." He may also have left his church, due to a "matter of principle." He exhibits a pattern of walking away from responsibility as a "matter of principle." I admit there are times when a principled decision is necessary, even admirable. But there are also times when that pattern reveals that no principle is at stake but wounded pride.

None of use likes to be treated unfairly. All of us desire relationships marked by mutual respect. But there are a lot of fools in the real world, and overreacting to their actions is to place them at the steering wheel of our lives.

Overreacting to authority can be dangerous. But equally dangerous is overrating ourselves if we are in places of authority. A marathoner's life is marked by humility, where every opportunity to lead is received gratefully and every position held loosely. I will never forget one of my early encounters with God. As a young pastor of a thriving congregation, I was feeling pretty good about "what I had caused to take place." I will never forget God's less than gentle rebuke:

"Wayne, I'm glad you are enjoying the place of leadership I have entrusted to you. I am glad you are using your gifts and sense me working through you. But never forget the lesson I taught Nebuchadnezzar years ago, when he surveyed his kingdom and assumed: 'Is not this the great Babylon I have built as the royal residence, by my mighty power and for the glory of my majesty?' (Daniel 4:30).

"I, God, sentenced him to seven years of insanity, during which he lived like a wild animal, until he concluded: 'Now I, Nebuchadnezzar, praise and exalt and glorify the King of heaven, because everything he does is right and all his ways are just. And those who walk in pride he is able to humble' (Daniel 4:37).

"Wayne, enjoy the blessings, lead with confidence, but never for a moment get your hands on my glory, or I will have you grazing in the fields for a while."

I have found it is safer to acknowledge gratefully that God has granted me a position he could have easily entrusted to someone else, rather than to convince myself I am indispensable. A marathoner must have God on his side, and God sides with humble people.

Memo #3: "Work Smarter, Not Harder"

The source of a man's effectiveness in life changes as the years go by. In his youth he can make an impact through sheer energy. Later on, as youthful vitality begins to dissipate, his ability to think strategically and his years of credibility are the major resources of his effectiveness. In that way, life is a bit like a game of squash. A friend of mine, a fine athlete who has played racquetball for years, has recently taken up squash. Being young and quick, he consistently loses to older and more experienced players. Their ability to anticipate and strategically place the ball more than overwhelms his quick reflexes. As time goes on, he will learn the game. So it is with life. A marathoner learns to work smarter, not harder. He learns to confine his risk:

Whoever digs a pit may fall into it;
* whoever breaks through a wall may be bitten by a snake.*
Whoever quarries stones may be injured by them;
* whoever splits logs may be endangered by them.* (10:8–9)

Any activity in life involves risk. A marathoner does not eliminate risks from his life, for so much of growth and new opportunity involves a measure of risk. It is certainly not wise to focus on past risks, reminiscing about the good old days. That is yesterday's news. A marathoner knows that the difference between wisdom and foolishness lies in risk analysis. It is a matter of determining the proper ratio of risk to reward. In the words of Chuck Swindoll, "There is a difference between inevitable risks and inexcusable stupidity."

If you were designing your financial portfolio, the first step would be identifying your "risk tolerance." You may be so risk-adverse that you naturally gravitate toward investments that may not even keep pace with inflation. On the other hand, you may be such a risk-taker that you tend to fall victim to "get-rich-quick" opportunities, forfeiting in a short while what has taken years to gain. Either extreme erodes effective results in long-term investing. So it is with life's marathon: If you never take a risk, you will fall off the pace. If you take unwarranted risks, you may undo years of accomplishment. Risks should be prayerfully considered. The input of others who know you well and know God well can be indispensable.

Another dimension to "working smarter, not harder" is the refinement of your skills:

If the ax is dull
  and the edge unsharpened,
more strength is needed
  but skill will bring success.
If a snake bites before it is charmed,
  there is no profit for the charmer. (10:10–11)

The first image is pretty obvious. A once-sharpened ax does not stay sharpened; rather, it dulls with use. You can compensate for its dullness by attempting to use more force, or you can stop and sharpen the ax.

The second image comes out of Eastern culture. Do not take your show on the road until you have charmed the snake. If the poisonous snake bites you or your customer, that will put an end to your business. Know your product before you market it!

Both images emphasize the need for staying sharp, the value of preparing thoroughly, and the requirement for intermittent learning. Stephen Covey uses the image of a factory and the formula of production capacity versus production. If a factory runs twenty-four hours a day, seven days a week, it may produce a great deal in a short time. But before long, without preventive maintenance, the machines will break down and long-term production is lost. On the other hand, if a company is always caring for its machines but never producing, those machines may have tremendous production capacity that is never utilized. In the midst of production there must be pauses for maintenance and fine-tuning.

You are so much more than a machine; you have been made in the image of God. Part of your design is that you need times of rest and refreshment. You need exercise for your body and enrichment for your mind. Long-term effectiveness means monitoring your "production capacity" as well as producing results.

The writer of Ecclesiastes is not negating the value of hard work. Any marathoner realizes some segments of a race require extra effort. You exert more energy climbing a hill or gasping for the proverbial second wind. Thoughtfulness will never compensate for laziness! Working smarter, however, means your energy is carefully focused to make the maximum contribution toward the long-term goal.

Many years ago a mathematician named Pareto conceived what later became known as the 80/20 rule. He stated that 80 percent of the results come from 20 percent of the effort, and the remaining 20 percent of the results come from the remaining 80 percent of the effort. The ability to discern which efforts lead to the greatest results is prerequisite to working smarter.

A businessman with whom I am acquainted needed to reduce expenses in his company in order for his business to survive, let alone thrive. He discovered that while his business served over twenty clients, 90 percent of his business came from just six of them. Yet it was incredibly expensive for him to maintain services to the nearly twenty customers who provided just 10 percent of his business. He decided to focus the company's energy and expenses on the six major clients. While continuing to relate respectfully to the remaining clients, he made sure that if they requested additional services, they would pay additional expenses. Working smarter, not harder, may have saved his company.

He came to those conclusions about his business after doing some reading, reflecting, analyzing, and conversing with knowledgeable friends. He spent time in prayer. He stopped to sharpen the ax. You must too! Whether it's building a business, a marriage, or your personal future, some time-outs are required.

"Work smarter, not harder" also applies in the arena of relationships. For instance, I have noticed that husbands and wives say and receive love in different ways. A man may work hard to let his wife know he loves her, yet may not be communicating in a way that is meaningful to her. He "says" love by seeking to be a good provider; she "hears" love when he takes the time to listen to her. He "says" love by buying her nice presents; she "hears" love when he is considerate enough to pick up after himself. It is a wise man who learns how his wife "hears" that he loves her.

Otherwise, you exhaust yourself communicating love in ways that do not connect with her. Work smarter.

Memo #4: "Don't Believe Your Own P. R."

A marathoner is capable of matching his walk with his talk:

Words from a wise man's mouth are gracious,
  but a fool is consumed by his own lips.
At the beginning his words are folly;
  at the end they are wicked madness—
  and the fool multiplies words. (10:12–14a)

The writer of Ecclesiastes is describing a man who is becoming consumed with his own words. He is mesmerized by his own speech. At some point he begins to believe his own P. R., and what starts out as folly degenerates into wicked madness. And he just keeps talking!

We all know people with the gift of gab. In the beginning this can be a great benefit. Some men have talked themselves into impressive positions. Their way with words opened doors. We also know that if their sales pitches are not reinforced by a good work ethic and performance record, those words ring hollow. A strength in verbal presentation becomes a weakness when substituted for good follow-through. "If you talk the talk, you start quickly but finish poorly. If you walk the walk, you may start more slowly but finish strongly."

One year I was mentored by Dr. Russell Mawby, then CEO of the W. K. Kellogg Foundation. Russ rarely mentioned whom he knew and where he had been unless it related to a principle or experience he was sharing with me. I only learned from others that he regularly rubbed shoulders with some of the nation's top political leaders, academicians, and businesspersons. He spent his time with me talking about his vision, about what others were doing, and about causes in which he believed. He had a right to boast, but didn't. He stands out in a world of men who have no right to boast, but do!

Try to say less and live more. This is a marathoner's strategy.

THE FINISH LINE

Here are some mile markers you will want to watch for in the process of your life's marathon:

God is doing a marathon work in you. He began before you were born, and he has a plan for all your days (Psalm 139:13–16). He will help you lay foundations on which you can build. He will redeem the uphills and downhills of your life for your ultimate good. He will refine you inside and out by the continual work of his Spirit. Commit your life to him and be confident "that he who began a good work in you will carry it on to completion until the day of Christ Jesus" (Philippians 1:6).

Make the most of the stages of manhood. The Bible makes it clear that you are to grow up. You begin as a boy. You mature into a man, not only physically, but emotionally, socially, and spiritually. You become a husband, and in the process of marriage you discover a whole new set of opportunities for growth! You become a father and are both delighted and frightened that you see a lot of yourself in your children! You become a "patriarch"–the biblical word for a man who has influence on subsequent generations (grandchildren and great-grandchildren) and the surrounding community. We live in a society where "men are boys with more expensive toys." Marathon men grow up and take responsibility for their ever-increasing ripples of influence.

Check your motives. Men run physical marathons for a variety of reasons–personal fitness, competition with others, to prove something to themselves, to better their previous time, to prove something to others, and the list goes on. What motivates you to do what you do and say what you say? Life marathoners who finish strongest have motives that are intricately interwoven with the eternal purposes of God.

Watch your pace. Many men start their lives with high expectations for personal growth, family life, career accomplishment, and spiritual vitality. They welcome accountability from others as they stretch toward initial goals. All too often, as time goes on, men trade their expectations for excuses. They convince themselves that they deserve "freedom" rather than remaining accountable. They drop off the pace and fail to finish strongly.

Furthermore, many men "rev" their engines so high during their careers that in retirement their engines shut down. Pace yourself throughout life. Schedule in "refreshment stops" along the way and have something left to share with others.

Learn from other marathoners who are ahead of you. One of the men I keep an eye on is Joe Stowell, president of Moody Bible Institute. I do not know him personally, but I read his writings regularly. When he turned fifty, he penned these words:

> There was a time when my life was far too fast. When I was too busy gaining on my dreams to properly value my friends. Not anymore. Those few who have loved and accepted me through the years regardless of my several faults are great treasures indeed.

I am learning that very few things are really important. Only things like truth, a clear conscience, laughter, giving, serving, and a faithful dog ultimately count.

A quieter, more reflective life. More time to read and grow. The love of my wife, Martie. Deeper intimacy with Christ. These are what occupy my dreams and desires these days.

I find myself often thinking about that little phrase that used to be so common among God's people, "Only one life, 'twill soon be past, only what's done for Christ will last."[2]

Develop a list of people who are marathoners just ahead of you in years and personal development. Learn from their lives.

Make retirement decisions prayerfully, not selfishly. Some men reach the apex of their influence and then walk away in early retirement. Bob Buford is right when he says our approach to the second half of life should be different, but don't walk off the platform that your years of influence have created. Stay in the game. Invest your credibility to accomplish things everlastingly worthwhile. Don't move away from the area where you are known and abandon the network you have created in the name of "enjoying your retirement." That may be a selfish and ultimately unsatisfying decision.

Don't believe the myths of aging. Many men assume diminishing capacities to learn and change as they age, and they act on those assumptions. *U.S. News and World Report* exposed several myths about brain power as a person ages:[3]

Myth	Truth
1. It only gets worse	1. You are not inevitably destined for a steep mental decline. A third of people over seventy function as well as ever.
2. Memory is the first to go	2. Your store of facts and procedures should be unaffected by age, but your capacity for abstract reasoning may fade over time.
3. Use it or lose it	3. Yes, up to a point. But simply engaging in a boring or repetitive mental activity will not stave off decline. Pursue eclectic interests.
4. Sound body, sound mind	4. Physical health does not always assist the vigor of your intellect; sometimes exercise that is too intense may hurt your mental abilities.
5. You can't teach an old dog new tricks	5. An old brain can rewire itself to compensate for losses, and refresher courses can keep your mind sharp.

Keep learning and growing!

Know where the finish line is. Where is the finish line for life's marathon? Where is the awards banquet? Bill Gates, CEO of Microsoft and one of the world's wealthiest men, was asked, "What's next to shoot for?" He responded, "If I had some set idea of a finish line, don't you think I would have crossed it years ago?" Like Gates, you may not know the finish line of your business endeavor, but you must consider the finish line of life.

If you are a Christian, you know where the finish line is. You know where the awards banquet will be held. The ultimate "Well done" that you live for will not come from your spouse or your employer; it will come in heaven as you stand before Christ. The apostle Paul encourages you to build with that reality in view:

> *For no one can lay any foundation other than the one already laid, which is Jesus Christ. If any man builds on this foundation using gold, silver, costly stones, wood, hay or straw, his work will be shown for what is, because the Day will bring it to light. It will be revealed by fire, and the fire will test the quality of each man's work. If what he has built survives, he will receive his reward. If it is burned up, he will suffer loss; he himself will be saved, but only as one escaping through flames.* (1 Corinthians 3:11–15)

The great apostle realized his salvation was not dependent on his works. He also knew the contribution of his life would ultimately be evaluated and rewarded in the stadium of heaven, not by the fickle audiences of earth. As another great writer of Scripture put it:

> *Therefore, since we are surrounded by such a great cloud of witnesses, let us throw off everything that hinders and the sin that so easily entangles, and let us run with perseverance the race marked out for us. Let us fix our eyes on Jesus, the author and perfecter of our faith.* (Hebrews 12:1–2a)

Loading a life without long-range vision is like driving a car while looking only in the rearview mirror and occasionally checking the fuel gauge. No long-range vision is complete unless it catches a glimpse of the halls of heaven.

NOTES

1. *Detroit Free Press* (May 5, 1995).
2. *Moody Monthly* (September, 1994).
3. *U.S. News and World Report* (November 28, 1994), pp. 89–97.

11

Leaning Into Life

SCRIPTURE: ECCLESIASTES 11:1–6

John Maxwell is an insightful proponent of the value of leadership, especially spiritual leadership. His conferences are inspirational and brimming with nuggets worth considering and acting upon. Here is one:

With momentum, leaders look better than they actually are.

Without momentum, leaders look worse than they actually are.

With momentum, followers increase their performance.

Without momentum, followers decrease their performance.

John believes momentum is the greatest of all change agents and that no leader can afford to overlook its importance. Many times momentum is the only difference between a winning, positive growth climate and a losing, negative growth climate.

Look at the climate of your life. Are you gaining momentum in the direction you desire, or do you feel as if you are losing ground on those things you ultimately value? Is your spiritual life deepening and pervading every dimension of your life, or do you feel as if God and you are in a rut? Is your marriage becoming more intimate, or are you going through the motions, peacefully coexisting? In the words of Bob Buford, is your life moving from success to significance, or do your accomplishments seem more superficial than ever?

What creates the "big mo" (momentum)? You might think it is the forks in the road—those decisive, defining moments where life-altering decisions need to be made. And in the course of your life you will certainly encounter those dramatic "choice points." But more often, momentum is a result of a series of smaller decisions. These successive steps, insignificant if isolated from one another, together form a momentum that sets the direction of your life. They require everyday decisions and daily faithfulness. Those who lead best have this attitude: "I know we need to change, but I know it is not magic, or inspiration. It's completing many, many undramatic small steps successfully."[1]

I see men all the time who have ignored the little things that are so important to their marriages until a crisis erupts. Or they neglect daily spiritual disciplines until God seems distant. They come to me seeking a quick fix to reverse the snowball effect of their action or inaction.

A great athlete reaches the top of his game by consistently training his body and incrementally refining his skills. A person earns an academic degree by charting each semester and completing it one class at a time. A good employee (or boss) daily seeks to work hard, treat people with dignity, and keep learning the little things that produce growth.

Lean into life. Decide clearly and specifically what you want. Be honest with yourself, with others, and with God. Take risks that are appropriate and take responsibility for your choices. Commit to doing what it takes and fully participate in everything you do.

The writer of Ecclesiastes had momentum in mind when he penned chapter 11 of his journal. Here are some of the principles that he promotes.

BE PROACTIVE RATHER THAN PROTECTIVE

Using illustrations from his world, the Teacher describes how to get the ball rolling:

Cast your bread upon the waters,
 for after many days you will find it again.
Give portions to seven, yes to eight,
 for you do not know what disaster may come upon the land. (11:1–2)

He is encouraging us to take a risk, to go for it!

I am convinced that when most men think about risk, their minds connect it with their business or finances. True, these verses encapsulate a solid investment strategy. To increase your net worth you must do some investing—"Cast your bread upon the waters." Wise investing involves diversification, resisting the temptation to put all your eggs in one basket—"Give portions to seven, yes to eight." Diversification is a way of reducing the downside risk that may occur with reversals in one segment of the market—"You do not know what disaster may come upon the land."

But the application of these verses can be broadened, for there are other risks worth taking and investments worth making:

- The risk of sharing Christ with an unbelieving friend
- The risk of building a few true friendships rather than dozens of acquaintances
- The risk of talking about your personal story – how you have been hurt and where you are growing
- The risk of ministering to several others, even though it may make a difference for only one or two
- The risk of admitting to your children you are not perfect and will need forgiveness from time to time, but you want to be the best parent possible

Broaden your investment strategy to include your relationships with others and with God. Investing financially may bring success, but investing relationally will bring significance to your life.

The writer of Ecclesiastes gives advice that goes against our natural tendencies. When we are uncertain about a situation ("you do not know what disaster may come upon the land"), we tend to become cautious and protective. A "rainy day mentality" takes hold. Financially, many people feel like withdrawing from the stock market when it is struggling and investing in the stock market when it is surging. As a result, they sell "low" and buy "high." Their feelings lead them to do the exact opposite of conventional wisdom: Buy "low" and sell "high."

The same phenomenon occurs relationally. When you feel uncertain about your relationship with your wife, there is a tendency to withdraw. At the very time you need to be open about your concerns and proactive in expressing your love, you become protective. It requires great faith to be vulnerable with your wife at the time when your natural feelings are screaming for you to close up.

It is also true of your relationship with God. When you feel uncertain about where he is leading you, you tend to take the reins of your life out of his hands. At the very moment that faith requests you trust him more, your feelings are encouraging you to trust yourself.

It is one of the great paradoxes of life. "One man gives freely, yet gains even more; another withholds unduly, but comes to poverty" (Proverbs 11:24). In the words of Jesus, "Whoever finds his life will lose it, and whoever loses his life for my sake will find it" (Matthew 10:39). If you selfishly guard your interests, your world becomes smaller and your future dimmer. If you generously invest yourself in others and in God, your influence grows and your future becomes eternally brighter.

Many men have chosen to "close their spirit" rather than be open; the hurt and disappointments of life have created a protective shell. But by opening your spirit little by little, you allow God and others in. You permit your true self to show; you find the life God came to give you.

A man who allowed me to glimpse "behind the scenes" of his life revealed his upbringing had led him to build high walls around his heart until it became the unconquerable fortress. These walls were reinforced and heightened by decades of addiction to alcohol. Through an A.A. group, the walls have begun to come down, and honesty is replacing secrecy. As he began to think about his relationship with God, his attitude was reflected in this question: "How much of the world can I hang on to, and how much control can I keep, and still get satisfaction from God?"

While his background is unique, I am convinced his question is one all of us ask. If I give God a corner of my life, a few hours of my week, will that be enough to get the blessing from him that I want? The answer is no. If you give God a portion, what you want will change. He will transform your desires. As you give away more and more to him and to others, "after many days you will find it again."

Not only is this openness a necessity in relationships, it is a must for leadership. When our church first began, I knew everyone and everything. But as the church started to grow, there were individuals I no longer recognized. People began to ask questions about our ministry for which I had no answer. A decision to be more controlling, to keep things at a level I was comfortable with, would have stymied the outreach of our ministry. I had to let go, to delegate. I had to "cast bread upon the waters." I had to "give portions" of responsibility and authority to others.

But there is a time period after you have made your investment that requires faith and trust. The return does not come immediately, but "after many days." I remember those uncomfortable days of "letting go," while my feelings were screaming to "hang on" and the benefits were not yet apparent. I was bemoaning my dilemma to a dear older saint in our congregation who lovingly confronted me by saying, "Wayne, I know you miss knowing some of the people, and some of us miss being close to you. But never forget that it is more important that people know Jesus than know you." That was the heart of the matter, that the investment of my leadership in others would bring the satisfaction of introducing people to Christ. "Cast your bread upon the waters. . . . Give portions to seven or eight."

A leader I greatly respect, Dr. Joe Seaborn, is constantly upgrading the quality of his ministry. He does not ask, "What is the one dramatic thing I can do to revolutionize my life?" but instead, "What are the seven or eight little steps I can make to take my leadership up a notch or two?" They may not all make a difference, but a few of them will.

So I ask you, "What are the seven or eight areas you need to give attention to? What will take your relationship with God up a notch? What will move your relationship with your wife to a more intimate level? What will lift your career to the next step?" Momentum requires an adventuresome spirit, truly open to God and others.

STOP DRIFTING, START DECIDING

Some men spend their whole lives observing the obvious and inspecting the inevitable. They continually toy with the maybes and the might-have-beens as they drift through life. They suffer from a form of paralysis described as follows:

If the clouds are full of water,
    they pour rain upon the earth.
Whether a tree falls to the south or to the north,
    in the place where it falls, there will it lie.
Whoever watches the wind will not plant;
    whoever looks at the clouds will not reap. (11:3–4)

In a poetic way the writer of Ecclesiastes reminds us that certain dimensions of life are inevitable and uncontrollable. You must learn to read the signs and recognize the conditions, but don't get caught watching instead of acting.

1. Don't Let Your Decisions Be Controlled by Conditions

If you spend your whole life waiting for the ideal opportunity, it may never come. If you search for just the right moment, it may never come. Sometimes you just need to plant the seed and move ahead, even if the rain comes and the wind is blowing. Many men buy into what I have labeled the "perfect conditions" myth. For Christian men, it goes like this: "If it is God's will, the conditions will be perfectly conducive to moving ahead. If it is God's work, things will work out perfectly."

No, many things that are God's will take place in less than perfect conditions. He uses imperfect conditions to test our faith and faithfulness. He uses imperfect conditions to refine our character—to remove the rough edges and purify our motives. He uses imperfect conditions to keep us humble by reminding us of the many aspects of any situation we cannot control. God will accomplish his perfect will in you under less than perfect conditions.

Think about it for a moment:

- If you wait for the perfect time and place to read your Bible and pray, how often will you have quiet times with God? Once a month?
- If you wait for the perfect ministry opportunity that utilizes all of your gifts and eliminates all your frustrations, will you ever be involved in ministry?
- If you wait for the perfect cause before you give, will you ever give?
- If you wait for the perfect church led by the perfect pastor before you commit yourself to it, will you ever join?

"Whoever watches the wind will not plant"; some of the seed he scatters might not land exactly where he intended. "Whoever looks at the clouds will not reap"; it might rain and a damp harvest will mildew in storage. Ecclesiastes is not saying we should plant in a windstorm or harvest in a rainstorm, for we are to use common sense! But over-analysis leads to indecision.

The church I serve as pastor concluded some time ago that God was leading us to build a new sanctuary to accommodate our growing church family and to welcome new people from our community. When we began our planning, the economy was weak, but interest rates were falling and building prices were stable. As we continued our planning, the economy grew stronger; but at the same time, interest rates began to rise and building prices increased. It was tempting to believe that if God was in this step of faith, conditions would be perfect–a growing economy, full employment and higher wages for our membership, low interest rates, rock-bottom construction costs, and people lining up to pledge and give. But we determined that conditions would never be perfect. We must consider the economic environment but not be controlled by it. What we do, we must do in response to God, not in response to perfect conditions.

2. Don't Let Your Decisions
Be Controlled by Assumptions

Any good strategic planning process begins with the surfacing of assumptions. Making decisions and building momentum based on wrong assumptions just takes you in the wrong direction fast!

When I sit down with a couple for premarital counseling, I review a questionnaire I have had them complete in advance of our appointment. Some of the questions relate to the quality of their parents' marriages, what made these marriages good or bad, how their parents resolved conflict, and how they communicated. This is more than a gossip session about their parents! I have found that a couple makes assumptions about their own marriage based on the marriages of their parents. Assumptions (based on how things have been) take the place of decisions (based on how they would like things to be) as the foundation of their relationship. Imagine the potential for conflict:

- If one partner grew up in a home where the dad managed the finances, while the other partner lived in a home where mom kept the books and gave dad an "allowance"
- If one partner grew up in a home with a strong-willed dad and weak-willed mom, while the other lived in a home with a strong-willed mom and a weak-willed dad
- If one partner grew up in a home where the parents did everything together, while the other lived in a home where each parent pursued his or her own interests.

Unless such assumptions are faced and decisions made, I will be seeing a couple like this for after-marriage counseling before the first year of marriage is completed!

Many men fail to recognize the impact of assumptions. As one entrepreneur wisely observed, his whole company was based on just a few assumptions, assumptions that impacted everything from financial projections to customer service. Those assumptions had better be right, for the future of his business depended on it.

If you are forming a business partnership, talk thoroughly and discuss completely your assumptions. If you are considering marriage, do the same—as with parenting, volunteering, retiring, and so forth. Good communication is the only prescription for surfacing assumptions.

3. Don't Let Your Decisions Be Controlled by Past Patterns

Closely related to the danger of assumptions is the unconscious continuation of life as it has always been. The rallying cry is, "We've never done it that way before." We are creatures of habit and develop comfort zones that lead to repetitive patterns of thinking and acting.

These past patterns are powerful and contribute to momentum. If the patterns are good, it is easy to generate momentum toward good decisions and behaviors. But if these patterns are dysfunctional, momentum inclines us toward unhealthy ways of responding to life. The power of these patterns can continue for generations.

Often the patterns are subconscious, conditioning our responses without our awareness. They have been described as the "old tapes" that we play over and over; though rooted in our past, they influence our present and future. Thus, a man may yell at his kids not because the present situation warrants yelling, but because his dad yelled at him. A man may suppress his feelings (though his wife would love to hear what is going on deep inside of him), because he was never allowed to express his feelings while growing up.

As these patterns gain momentum and strength, they can create a vicious cycle. Change never comes easily, especially if you feel you are the victim and bear no responsibility for reversing the pattern. Some patterns can be altered by sheer willpower. Some require additional insight from a counselor. Sometimes accountability to another man or a small group is necessary. At times all of these in the hands of our gracious and powerful God are a must.

It is easier and more comfortable to continue in set patterns than to reverse them. Perspective is developed when you weigh the risk of reversing patterns with the risk of doing things the same old way. Confronting counterproductive patterns can take heroic effort but have benefits not only for you, but for generations to come.

Good decisions require us to choose consciously what we wish to continue and what we wish to change. The

───────────── **197** ─────────────

changes will likely occur through a series of small victories. Don't underestimate the momentum that even a small, new beginning can generate. One area in which I have noticed this principle at work is generosity: "It is relatively easy to change a little giver into a bigger giver. It is much more difficult to change a nongiver into a giver."

Men will come to me, aware of a financial need in a ministry, and say, "If I have record sales this year, I will meet that need." Or, "If I win the lottery, I will meet that need." I often feel like asking, "Are you giving now?" If the answer is "No," I do not expect to see a dime if their business had a banner year or if they won the largest jackpot ever. Giving has everything to do with a person's character and track record and little to do with one's account balance.

4. Don't Let Your Decisions Be Controlled by Rationalization

We have infinite ability to live in denial and shift responsibility to others. We can rationalize our inaction as well as our poor decisions. Finger-pointing and scape-goating are highly enjoyable but nonproductive behaviors. In the words of Ecclesiastes, I can avoid planting by rationalizing "the wind might blow"; I can justify failing to harvest by rationalizing that "it might rain."

Stop drifting and start deciding. Inaction and passivity are not acceptable in any arena of life. I have counseled with some extremely frustrated wives whose husbands are decisive at work but passive at home. When a problem arises at the office, they face it, diagnose it, and resolve it. When a problem arises at home, they are disinterested and shun responsibility. When it comes to decisiveness, work gets the main course and home gets the leftovers—if there is anything left. There are wives who have a deep longing for their husbands to exercise at home just a fraction of the leadership they exhibit at work.

Here are some dimensions of decisiveness:

1. Little decisions mean a lot. I have noticed there is plenty of literature on strategically formulating major decisions, but developing the skill of making little decisions with a long-term horizon is equally important.

2. Learn the value of predeciding. This means anticipating situations that may arise and require your response. This is a particularly powerful practice when it comes to temptation. Decide in advance to avoid certain settings. Predecide what you will say to a person who makes you an offer you cannot refuse but should. Spur-of-the-moment decisions in tempting situations are perilous.

3. Transcend pettiness in deciding what is best. It is amazing how territorial or vengeful we can become, especially if we are bitterly disappointed. Many bright futures have been sacrificed on the altar of pettiness. "Teaching someone else a lesson" is a life mission statement that will honor neither you nor God.

4. Some decisions are "tough calls." Like the umpire in a game, you may not have the best vantage point or get it right every time, but you have to make the call.

Years ago I attended a conference at the Crystal Cathedral in southern California. One of the speakers was W. Clement Stone, then a businessman in the Midwest. I do not remember the subject of his talk that day, but I do recall one phrase he used repeatedly: "Do it now!" It was his answer to a life adrift.

COMMIT INSTEAD OF CONTEMPLATE

The writer of Ecclesiastes notes two final impediments to momentum. One is our limited understanding:

As you do not know the path of the wind,
or how the body is formed in a mother's womb,
so you cannot understand the work of God,
the Maker of all things. (11:5)

This verse brings to mind a bit of graffiti that contained above average theology: "A God who is small enough to fit in your mind isn't big enough to meet your needs." God's creativity and capability are endless. His ways are worth considering and following. Rather than "twisting God's arm" in prayer to get him to do things your way, it is vital to understand his ways and then to align yourself with his purposes.

This verse is not an excuse for sloppy thinking. "I just don't understand" can be a flimsy substitute for not wrestling with the deeper issues of faith. But if you live only by what you understand, you will not live a full life. Some of God's "above the sun" ways are beyond us. Once you understand all that, you can, you must move ahead while trusting God for what is not yet understood. At times you must invest energy even when there is uncertainty. That is part of living by faith, not by sight.

I have seen men whose momentum stalls in their walk with God because of encountering a situation they cannot understand. They stop in their tracks to reflect on what God may be up to. In moderation, this can be beneficial. But many times you will have to proceed without complete understanding. In fact, there are many things

God does not show us until *after* we have faithfully followed that which we do understand. We say, "God, show me your path, and I will walk in it." He says, "Start walking, and the path will become clear."

Some men stall because of trying to understand what cannot be understood. Yet others stall as they seek a guarantee that their attempt will be successful:

Sow your seed in the morning,
  and at evening let not your hands be idle,
for you do not know which will succeed,
  whether this or that,
  or whether both will do equally well. (11:6)

There are no guarantees. Be faithful, start early, and keep at it, even though you do not know if, when, where, or how it will make a difference.

Ecclesiastes is redefining success. God measures success by faithful efforts, not fantastic results. We do the planting; he determines the harvest. Like most men, I have offered to switch roles with God: He can do the planting, and I will handle the harvest. He has never taken me up on that offer, and I suspect he never will.

Success is being faithful to God's calling in your life. If he has called you to build a business and you faithfully pursue that calling, you are equally successful if the business never gets off the ground or it becomes a Fortune 500 company. If he calls you to be a father and you faithfully fulfill your responsibilities, you are a success no matter what life choices your children ultimately make. Success is determined by what you "sow," not by what you "reap."

When Kentwood Community Church began in 1979, I organized an initial door-to-door canvass in our community. During that summer, we knocked on literally thousands of doors. As near as we could tell, only three families from those visits became part of the core of our church. That is, less than one-tenth of one percent responded initially. Those early years of our church were challenging. Then, in 1983, we moved into our first church building. To our surprise, our church doubled in attendance in just one week. Did I anticipate that knocking on thousands of doors would result in just a few families responding? No. Did I anticipate that just opening the doors of a new church building would cause attendance to double immediately? No. "For you do not know which will succeed, whether this or that, or whether both will do equally well." As much as you would like to predict the results of your efforts, ultimately which efforts will succeed is known only by God.

Whether you will live generously and adventurously has everything to do with your worldview. If you must understand everything and be assured of success before you take a risk, you will never venture far. If you leave ultimate understanding and the measuring of success to the counsel of God, you can go for it. In the words of one man's response to this truth, "I have to decide whether I'll try to play God or I'll work God's plan."

You do not know what will succeed and what will fail. Studies indicate that while success and failure appear to be polar opposites, the fear of failure and the fear of success have similar roots. I have a friend who finally came to realize that the very skills he had developed to combat failure he also used to sabotage success! As he began to focus less on results (success or failure), and more on his character as well as core commitments, he experienced a personal paradigm shift. Rather than being driven to fight "failure" and being uncomfortable with "success," he focused on being faithful to his life's mission. He managed the sowing; now he is working on letting God manage the harvest.

APPROPRIATE AMBITION

Finally, this portion of the Ecclesiastes journal is a call to be ambitious. Let's hear the Teacher's challenges again:

"Cast your bread upon the waters."

"Give portions to seven, yes to eight."

"Sow your seed in the morning, and at evening let not your hands be idle."

Don't wait until you have it all figured out or until success is guaranteed. Go for it.

Ambition has received a bum rap. We are suspicious of someone who is ambitious and in the process may have settled for far less of life than God would like to give. Granted, there is a form of raw ambition that is selfish and turned inward. Jesus spoke of this in Luke 12 in the story of a man who responded to God's blessing of an abundant harvest by building bigger barns and keeping it all for himself. Ambition that results in nothing more than bigger barns (or bigger houses, bigger cars, bigger companies) is selfish and condemned by God.

But what about ambition that is focused outward and benefits others as well as yourself? What about ambition that is focused upward and benefits the kingdom of God? That is, what about the following ambitions:

- To love your wife as Christ loves the church (Ephesians 5:25–33)
- To be an earthly father who prepares his children for a relationship with their heavenly Father
- To create a work environment where employees experience the justice and mercy God requires
- To build influence through which others may be led to consider a commitment to Christ

I challenge you to extend your ambition beyond the bottom lines of business and career. Be ambitious in your pursuit of loving others and loving God.

NOTES

1. Murray M. Dalziel and Stephen C. Schoonover, *Changing Ways* (New York: AMACOM, 1988), p. 14.

12

Taking It to the Limits

SCRIPTURE: ECCLESIASTES 11:7–12:12

Greek mythology contains the fable of Icarus, where creativity led to his destruction. Having fashioned wings from wax and feathers, he soared into the heavens. As he rose higher and higher, the sun melted the wax of his wings, and he plunged to his death in the Aegean Sea.

One management book refers to this as "The Icarus Paradox." The power of Icarus's wings stimulated a sense of abandon that led to his downfall. His greatest asset became his ultimate liability. In the corporate world, many outstanding companies allow their strengths to seduce them into excesses that cause their descent into mediocrity. In the personal world, many men fail to recognize the limits that will enable their continued success.

In part, this is due to our tendency to view limits as a restriction rather than as protection. This tendency reveals itself early in life, even in childhood. A parent tries to teach his or her child, "The stove is hot, so don't touch it." The child finds it hard to trust the parent's greater wisdom and experience; as a result, he "gets burned" before he sees the value of the limits. Unfortunately, we do not outgrow this tendency; as men we often "get burned." We do not trust the ultimate wisdom and eternal experience of our heavenly Father. We are not convinced that his loving limits are protective rather than restrictive.

Part of being "creature" and not the Creator is living within limits. The key to "top of the line" living is accepting God's limits as a demonstration of his love. You must trust that he will do what is best for you and keep you from what harms you. You must learn his limits and receive them as an act of grace rather than an act of law. You must respond to them early before being burned by the consequences of crossing his boundaries for you. Early response helps you avoid needless trauma to God's design for you. Learn the warning signals and develop a sensitivity to God's Spirit. You will thereby avoid a world of heartache.

A helpful book I recommend to men is *Running the Red Lights.*[1] It helps men face their sexual temptations and take preventive measures to keep them from violating God's limits by committing adultery. Affairs do not just happen; several warning signals must be ignored along the way. So many men dwell on the fantasy of "the grass is greener" that they deliberately tune out God's overtures to their consciences. I see the "behind-the-scenes" results of the immense brokenness as they learn only too late of the devastation that comes by exceeding the limits. If they had only trusted God's loving limits!

Men struggling with addiction speak of needing to "hit bottom" before they will change. "Hitting bottom" comes at different points for different men. Some lose their jobs before they wake up. Some lose their families. Some lose their health. Some have to lose it all. Some never do face reality. Life without limits becomes life without a future.

The struggle with God's limits is as old as Adam and Eve. God warned them it would be best if they did not eat of that one particular tree in the garden, though they were welcome to enjoy all the rest. They convinced themselves that God's limit was unwarranted and that they could be "like God." Throughout history we have lived with the consequences of their choice.

Limits are like the banks of a river. Those banks give the river depth, direction, movement, and power. Without banks, you have nothing more than a swamp. Overflow the banks, and you have a flood capable of great destruction. God has set limits to your life to keep you flowing with force toward his best for you.

The writer of Ecclesiastes concludes his journal by listing a series of invitations God gives and the limits he has established:

Invitation	Limitation
• Enjoy every day and every dimension of life	• You are accountable for every day and dimension of life
• Experience a life that is free of worry	• Serenity comes as you respond to your Creator's design for your life
• Think creatively and search actively for the meaning of life	• Be responsive to the truth of God's Word by learning and obeying it

It comes down to a test of trust. God invites us to experience an in-bounds life in an out-of-bounds world.

CULTIVATE YOUR DESIRES
WHILE REFLECTING GOD'S DESIGN

Whoever perpetuated the myth that God is against a good time has not read the last part of Ecclesiastes:

Light is sweet,
* and it pleases the eyes to see the sun.*
However many years a man may live,
* let him enjoy them all.*
But let him remember the days of darkness,
* for they will be many.*
* Everything to come is meaningless.*
Be happy, young man, while you are young,
* and let your heart give you joy in the days of*
* your youth.*
Follow the ways of your heart
* and whatever your eyes see.* (11:7–9a)

Now there's an invitation to enjoy life! The author says a man ought to enjoy every day of his life. "However many years a man may live, let him enjoy them all." Enjoyment has no age limit. Don't live in the past, hanging on to one stage of life and resisting entry into the next. Don't live for the future, hurrying into the next stage of life and missing the present. Enjoy every stage of life.

Several years ago I was handed a poem written by a fourteen-year-old boy, who had wisdom beyond his years.

PRESENT TENSE

It was spring, but it was summer I wanted,
The warm days, and the great outdoors.
* It was summer, but it was fall I wanted,*
The colorful leaves, and the cool, dry air.
* It was fall, but it was winter I wanted,*
The beautiful snow, and the joy of the holiday season.
* It was winter, but it was spring I wanted,*
The warmth, and the blossoming of nature.

I was a child, but it was adulthood I wanted,
The freedom, and the respect.
I was 20, but it was 30 I wanted,
To be mature, and sophisticated.
I was middle-aged, but it was 20 I wanted,
The youth, and the free spirit.
I was retired, but it was middle age I wanted,
The presence of mind, without limitations.
My life was over. But I never got what I wanted.

Jason Lehman

In other words, don't live your life never getting what you want because you convince yourself the best days are behind you or are yet to come. Enjoy every dimension of life, both the times that are brighter ("light is sweet") and the times that are darker ("remember the days of darkness"). I live in West Michigan. If I decide to enjoy only the days when the sun shines, I will enjoy only half of my life. Many people live only half of their lives because of a limited capacity to find joy and purpose in the "darker" moments. Every day may be beautiful in Mr. Rogers' neighborhood, but there are dreary ones in most other neighborhoods!

Your ability to "remember the days of darkness" will increase your capacity for contentment. Discontentment arises when you think only of the best times in life, of the best things other people have, and of the best possible scenarios of how things will work out. Facing the "days of darkness" builds appreciation for the lighter moments and tempers our expectations.

Be cautious about imagining too many sunny scenarios for the future. Many men live for the fantasy of early retirement, only to discover that this phase in which they expected every day to be bright has dark days as well. Without being too gloomy, I must recognize I may not live until retirement, or I may not have the health to enjoy retirement. I cannot bank too heavily on "good times to come"; I need to build some "mini-retirement times" in my life today through vacations, hobbies, and personal retreats.

The invitation is to enjoy life, but there is a limitation: "Know that for all these things God will bring you to judgment" (11:9). I am convinced that the interjection of "judgment" into this section is not meant to scare us. It is here to remind us that how we choose to enjoy our lives has consequences. Some of those consequences are immediate, while others become ultimately apparent at the judgment.

You and I are accountable for all our days and all the dimensions of life. A young person cannot say, "I'm young yet; I'll sow some wild oats and straighten it out with God when I'm older"; he is accountable now. An older person cannot say, "I've done my part; let someone else carry on while I just relax and enjoy myself"; he is still accountable to God. A person going through "dark days" cannot excuse disobedience because "God knows I'm going through a tough time." True, he knows about the tough times, and he gives the necessary grace for continued obedience.

God invites you to "rejoice responsibly" and not to forget your accountability beyond the moment and beyond yourself. Pat Williams, General Manager of the Orlando Magic and a committed Christian, observes that the typical man in our society seeks "maximum enjoyment while ignoring all restraints." God also invites you to maximum enjoyment and knows that enjoyment is deepest when you not only please yourself, but please God as well.

ELIMINATE YOUR WORRIES WHILE REMEMBERING YOUR CREATOR

The simple song "Don't Worry, Be Happy" rode to the top of the charts as it expressed the felt need of many people. We live in a worried world. The top-selling drugs, easily outpacing all others in volume of sales, are sedatives and ulcer medication. Medicating anxiety is a billion-dollar business. Here is the prescription of Ecclesiastes:

So then, banish anxiety from your heart
and cast off the troubles of your body,
for youth and vigor are meaningless.
Remember your Creator
in the days of your youth,
before the days of trouble come
and the years approach when you will say,
"I find no pleasure in them." (11:10–12:1)

"Banish anxiety from your heart." Don't worry, be happy. Eliminate it, don't medicate it.

There are plenty of reasons to worry, and the list grows longer as the years go by. The author of this book captures the litany of woes in word pictures.

Reference	Word Picture	Probable Meaning
12:2	"before the sun and the light and the moon and the stars grow dark"	the dimming of sight and senses as a person ages; night seems even darker
	"the clouds return after the rain"	one physical problem after another
12:3	"the keepers of the house tremble"	legs begin to get shaky

	"strong men stoop"	shoulders begin to hunch over
	"the grinders cease because they are few"	loss of teeth
	"those looking through the windows grow dim"	loss of eyesight
12:4	"when men rise up at the sound of birds"	tendency to get up early
	"all their songs grow faint"	loss of hearing
12:5	"afraid of heights and of dangers in the streets"	greater concern for safety; take less risks
	"the almond tree blossoms	hair gets white or gray
	"grasshopper drags himself along"	loss of leg strength (need for canes, walkers)
	"desire no longer is stirred"	loss of desire for food, drink, sex
	"goes to his eternal home"	death

This is a graphic description of the aging process!

The word "anxiety" is closely related to anger, resentment, and bitterness. Worry develops as you take responsibility for things you cannot control or change. As the anxiety builds, anger erupts or bitterness eats away at your heart. Men especially tend to mask their worries. I am reminded of a man who, hitting the limits of life, was diagnosed as a "raging" person. Further counseling unveiled the root problem as an "anxiety disorder." Men often rely on anger or hard work to hide the underlying anxiety from themselves and others.

"Banish anxiety ... cast off the troubles of your body, for youth and vigor are meaningless." It's a bit puzzling to unravel this line of thought, but Derek Kidner helps us:

> To idolize the state of youth and to dread the loss of it is disastrous: it spoils the gift even while we have it. To see it, instead, as a passing phase, "beautiful in its time" but not beyond it, is to be free from its frustrations.[2]

Just as youth does not automatically produce happiness, so aging does not automatically mean the loss of happiness. Don't overrate the "carefree" days of youth, and don't worry about the challenges of growing older.

How do we banish anxiety? "Remember your Creator in the days of your youth." That is, remember your Creator ASAP; don't postpone it. You will never be younger than you are today! Develop the pattern of remembering your Creator rather than a pattern of worrying about the coming realities of an aging person.

Remembering in the Bible means more than recalling something you have forgotten. It is more than a notation in your calendar or a stick-um note on your desk. It is not like "remember to pick up your dry cleaning" or even "remember your anniversary." Chuck Swindoll defines "remember" as a determination "to act decisively on behalf of someone."

One illustration of its use in Scripture centers around a couple who is infertile (still a common struggle among couples today). In 1 Samuel 1, Hannah goes to the temple to beg God for a child. She asks God to *remember* her (verse 11). Her prayers are so fervent that the priest Eli mistakenly assumes she is drunk. When she explains that she is simply emotional because of the depth of her desire for a child, the priest assures her God will answer her prayer. She returns home, has sexual relations with her husband, the Lord *remembers* her (verse 19), and she conceives and gives birth to a son. What, then, does it mean when the Bible says the "LORD remembered her"? Had God forgotten her and then something jogged his memory? No, God "acted decisively on her behalf."

To remember your Creator, therefore, is to act decisively on his behalf, to commit yourself to his purposes. That commitment dissipates worry.

Everyone has passing worries. It takes time to put things into perspective and adjust our attitudes. Worry can alert us to something that requires our attention and action. But if you are plagued by persistent anxiety, it is a sign that you do not trust God. You have not yet committed yourself to his purposes in the situation (acting decisively on his behalf).

It is not easy to remember your Creator. I have seen worried parents consistently rescue their grown children from the very consequences God may want to use to change them. I have seen a worried businessman tormented during an economic downcycle when God's purpose may be to humble him and reduce the priority that business has in his life. I have stood along the bedside of a man worried about his health when God may desire to take him home to heaven. Aligning our purposes with God's purpose will not happen effortlessly, but it will reduce anxiety.

*But seek first his kingdom and his righteous-
ness, and all these things will be given to you as
well. Therefore do not worry about tomorrow, for
tomorrow will worry about itself. Each day has
enough trouble of its own.* (Matthew 6:33–34)

These are Jesus' words as he echoes God's prescription for
anxiety: committing yourself to God's purposes.

The opposite of anxiety is serenity. You have undoubtedly read, and maybe even prayed, Reinhold Niebuhr's
classic prayer:

*God grant me the serenity
To accept things I cannot change,
Courage to change things I can,
And the wisdom to know the difference.*

This is a prayer about learning our limits and trusting God
for what is best. Worry-free living is not the result of
removing all responsibilities, but of fulfilling God-given
responsibilities.

STIMULATE YOUR MIND WHILE
RESPONDING TO GOD'S TRUTH

In 1989 the Millikin Corporation was presented the
highly coveted Malcolm Baldridge award. In commenting
on its pursuit of excellence, these foundational observations were offered:

1. Speed is only important when you are moving in
   the right direction.
2. Without data, you are just another person with
   an opinion.

These insights are an accurate summary of the journal of Ecclesiastes. As the author draws his search to a close, he recognizes the need to sort out God's truth from human speculation:

> *The Teacher searched to find just the right words, and what he wrote was upright and true.*
>
> *The words of the wise are like goads, their collected sayings like firmly embedded nails— given by one Shepherd. Be warned, my son, of anything in addition to them.*
>
> *Of making many books there is no end, and much study wearies the body.* (12:10–12)

There is a world of difference between the power of words inspired by God and the endless use of words by humans. To modify the Millikin Corporation's philosophy, "Without the wise words given by the one Shepherd (God himself), you are just another person with an opinion."

The Teacher warns us of the danger of additions to God's Word (12:12b). Most cults do not outwardly reject God's Word, but they offer new revelation that adds to (and claims final authority over) God's Word. Most cults are begun by founders disenchanted with the existing church and its beliefs, so they formulate distinctive doctrines to give them a new identify.

Individuals do the same. More than ever people are viewing God's Word like a buffet line in a restaurant, taking what they like—maybe a little bit of what is good for them—and leaving the rest for someone else. In effect, the diet a person receives is more a matter of what is palatable to them than what will truly nourish them.

God gives you his Word so that you might establish appropriate limits or boundaries in your life. I know of one businessman who reads through the Bible each year (he tends to fast forward through the genealogies, building plans for the tabernacles and temple, and some of the prophecies about ancient countries!) and tries to memorize at least one verse each month. While he sometimes feels a particular day's reading has yielded no new insight, he believes the cumulative effect of year-by-year reading through the Bible has nourished an eternal perspective. Out of that perspective comes his priorities and boundaries.

If God's truth does not set the banks of the river of your life, you tend to rely on your own intuition. Our opinions, however, are shaped by our experiences and may not be trustworthy. As one man put it,

> I grew up in a home where there was hardly any money. What little there was tended to be spent quickly, often on alcohol or pornography. In my adult years, I developed a successful career and a rather substantial income. No matter how much money came my way, I spent it fast. I had no normal parameters of financial discipline–no strategy for saving, spending, giving and no budget or long-term financial plans. It was not until I participated in a small group that specifically studied what the Bible says about money that I began to use it wisely. I learned what it means to exercise stewardship.

Do you hear what this man is saying? His own opinions were the result of his experience until he responded to God's truth.

This is not only true of proper parameters in the use of money. It is also true of the use of time, of ethical decisions, and of parenting practices. So many men "parent by pendulum"; that is, if their parents were strict, they tend to be lenient, whereas if their parents were lenient, they tend to be strict.

The truth of God's Word is "like firmly embedded nails." Have you ever been nailed by God's Word? Like a well-driven spike, it goes deep and is not easily removed. It penetrates your preconceived ideas. Perhaps this is why so many today want to relegate the Bible to a category of "ancient opinion" or believe that each individual is free to create his or her own interpretation of truth. Our society increasingly believes the axiom, "You have your truth, I have mine." We have lost a sense of the necessity of responding to God's truth. The words of Jesus, "I am the way and the truth and the life" (John 14:6), are now paraphrased to read, "I'll do it my way, conjure up my own concept of truth, and live my life as I please."

Perhaps another reason we are uncomfortable with the penetrating impact of God's words is that they have been used as weapons against us. Using a religious position to make additions to God's Word is nothing new, for Jesus faced the same dilemma. The Pharisees of his day had classified 613 commandments—248 positive, 365 negative (one negative command for each day of the year!). Some were great, some small; some were light, some heavy. No wonder a religious leader asked him, "Teacher, what is the greatest commandment in the Law?" (Matthew 22:34–40). If you had a "To Do" list hundreds of items long, you too would want to know where to begin! The religious leaders had added to God's Word, creating and reinforcing inappropriate limits. Their legalistic use of that Word turned off generations of people who might otherwise have been responsive to truth. Additions to Scripture can be used inappropriately to control others (legalism) or to control yourself (perfectionism).

As the truth of God's Word reaches your heart, you may be tempted to beat yourself up over past violations of his limits. You may wish you could start all over again. Like parents who finally get the hang of parenting as their kids go off to college, you may wish to go back to "square one." It is painful to have spent years climbing the ladder, only to learn that it is leaning against the wrong wall. But remember that God is redemptive. When we acknowledge our transgression of his limits, he forgives. "God can use what he does not choose." He has a miraculous ability to begin with us where we are. Don't be discouraged if you feel you have missed God's first choice for you—or his second choice, or even his third. Commit yourself to be responsive to his truth; welcome his Spirit of truth into the inner recesses of your heart.

Therefore, stimulate your mind with books, conversations, and the words of scholars and poets. But never forget that it is God's Word that refreshes your soul and redeems your life. Spiritual seeking at its best is not formulating your opinions, but responding to the words of the one Shepherd.

THE GOD OF "LOVING LIMITS"

There is a word in Russia that captures the chaos they are presently experiencing. From the land of *glasnost* and *perestroika* comes the concept of *bespredel*. Its literal translation is "no limits," and it is used to sum up the situation of a country where lawlessness is rampant. It is the nature of God our Creator to take what is formless and void (Genesis 1:2) and give it purpose. He uses "loving limits" to direct our lives graciously toward ultimate significance.

One of my favorite books in the Bible is Job. Job is a book about limits. It begins with God limiting the activity of Satan for Job's protection—just as God graciously protects us. While Job has a strong faith in God, he also has a fairly substantial ego. Job 13:15 captures both:

"Though he slay me, yet I will hope in him"—that's faith!
"I will surely defend my ways to his face"—that's ego!

How typically "male" of him to combine the two—faith and ego. God and me—we will whip this together. "God is my copilot" (as if God settles for anything less than the driver's seat!).

By the end of his difficulties, however, Job has learned his limits after encountering a limitless God:

My ears had heard of you,
  but now my eyes have seen you.
Therefore I despise myself
  and repent in dust and ashes. (Job 42:5–6)

Job ends his life as a spiritual giant. He has experienced God's protection as God limited the impact of evil on his life, he has experienced his own limits, and he has encountered a limitless God.

THE GOD OF LOVING LIMITS

> *It was you who set all the* boundaries *of the earth.* (Psalm 74:17)
> *Great is the Lord and mighty in power; his under-standing has* no limit. (Psalm 147:5)
> *For the one whom God has sent speaks the words of God, for God gives the Spirit* without limit. (John 3:34)

EPILOGUE

The last two verses of Ecclesiastes record "The Real Bottom Line":

TAKING IT TO THE LIMITS

Now all has been heard;
  here is the conclusion of the matter:
Fear God and keep his commandments,
  for this is the whole duty of man.
For God will bring every deed into judgment,
  including every hidden thing,
  whether it is good or evil. (12:13–14)

In the final analysis, the conclusion of the matter is verse 13: Whom are you going to fear? Whom or what will you reverence, respect, and serve? Who will become your master? The Teacher's search has surveyed many "masters": the pursuit of pleasure, the acquisition of knowledge, the accumulation of possessions—the list goes on. But there is only one Master worth serving: "Fear God and keep his commandments." Fear of God puts all other fears in place.

According to verse 14, nothing goes unnoticed and unassessed! God sees every hidden thing, even that which we try to hide from him or ourselves. No evil will go unpunished unless it is forgiven. No good will go unnoticed; the injustice of earth will be corrected in heaven.

Larry King, host of CNN *Nightline*, once asked Billy Graham, "Mr. Graham, are you an optimist or a pessimist?" To which the great evangelist replied, "I don't have an option. I'm a Christian." Everything is meaningless unless you search in the right places with the right perspective and pursue the real bottom line.

NOTES

1. Charles Mylander, *Running the Red Lights* (Ventura, Calif.: Regal Books, 1986).

2. Derek Kidner, *A Time to Mourn and a Time to Dance* (Downers Grove, Ill.: InterVarsity, 1976), p. 99.